Family Advocacy

FAMILY
ADVOCACY
A manual for action

Ellen Manser, editor

FAMILY SERVICE ASSOCIATION OF AMERICA
NEW YORK

International Standard Book Number: 0–87304–101–1
Library of Congress Catalog Card Number: 72–94392

Designed by Sheila Lynch

Printed in the United States of America

CONTENTS

INTRODUCTION

Family advocacy is not new to Family Service Association of America (FSAA) and its member agencies, but the name, the emphasis, and the effort to define and refine the purposes, goals, and methods of a family advocacy service have received increased attention in recent years. The impetus for this development has come from many sources, all related to the commitment of FSAA to be responsive to social conditions and to advances in methods of dealing with social problems. The family service movement has a well-earned reputation for its prominent role in over a century of developing and refining professional helping methods and applying them to the problems that were urgent and pressing at the time. The constant factor has been our purpose—the enrichment and strengthening of family life. Family advocacy shares this purpose.[1]

This manual has been prepared in response to a demand from member agencies for a rationale and guidelines to help interpret, plan, structure, and implement family advocacy services. It is difficult to meet all the needs of so diversified a group as the membership of a federation like FSAA in any single volume, no matter how lengthy. This manual clearly does not answer all the questions, but it does address itself

---

[1] See *Range and Emphases of a Family Service Program* (New York: Family Service Association of America, 1963).

in some measure to the major questions that have come from more than one or two agencies. It is designed as a basic reference for agencies presumed to be at various stages in their consideration or implementation of family advocacy services. It is not expected to substitute for individual consultations, staff development programs, or board-staff advocacy workshops, but it may be a useful tool in preparing for such activity.

The Contents page can guide the reader to those sections most pertinent to his immediate interest. Parts 2 and 3 include samples of member agency statements of purpose and policy, job descriptions, structure, and selected papers on advocacy subjects.

This manual is intended to reflect a developing concept. Our experience at FSAA and observation of member agency experience with advocacy has broadened and deepened the material gathered together in this volume to help administration, board, and staff members as they plan and work to serve families well in the 1970s. We expect that we will continue to learn so that future guidelines, policies, papers, and speeches on advocacy should again show modifications, expansion, rethinking. Because the concept of family advocacy is truly rooted in the best tradition and ethics of social work, much of what we have said and written in the past will remain valid and helpful even as methods to achieve our goals change and improve. This, then, is neither the first nor the last word on advocacy but a selective presentation of what we have been thinking and saying over a period of several years.

I am grateful to my colleagues at FSAA and a small group of member agency executives who responded thoughtfully and constructively to my request for their review of the first draft. I hope they will recognize many of their suggestions. Every response was carefully studied and each made a contribution, even if every possible amendment could not be fully adopted.

Family Service of Nassau County gave us the terms *family advocacy* and *case to cause*. Robert Sunley, associate director of the agency, was the first person to write his ideas about advocacy in a family agency and attempt to give guidance to family caseworkers on their roles in an advocacy agency. His papers and the agency's early reports of their program are valuable source material, and I hope my use of them in this manual will stimulate others with different ideas or experience to share the fruit of their thinking and their learning with the field through papers and reports.

Many member agencies have contributed through participation at FSAA Biennial Conferences, workshops, responses to questionnaires, program descriptions, committee deliberations, and case examples. To all who are working—too many to recognize individually—I take this opportunity to express admiration and appreciation.

I am heavily indebted to S. Frances Brisbane, advocacy director at FSAA from November 1969 to March 1971, not only for much of the content herein, but also for the inspiration her conviction and clarity of purpose have given me in the privileged position of working as her colleague in FSAA. Her brilliance and energy have set standards for the family advocacy program that challenge all who are exposed to her.

Finally, I am grateful to the administration of FSAA and particularly to Clark W. Blackburn, its general director, who has provided the solid base for change and given generously of his time, experience, and knowledge, thereby enabling the FSAA staff to explore, debate, make mistakes, learn, and do.

Family Advocacy

Part One

A Picture of Family Advocacy

DEFINITION

Family advocacy is a professional service designed to improve life conditions for people by harnessing direct and expert knowledge of family needs with the commitment to action and the application of skills to produce the necessary community change.[1] The purpose of family advocacy services is to insure that the systems and institutions with direct bearing on families work for those families, rather than against them.

Family advocacy goals include not only improvement of existing public and voluntary services and their delivery, but also development of new or changed forms of social services. Any institutionalized service such as housing, employment, welfare, education, health care, recreation, transportation, police and courts, and social agencies including family service agencies may be in need of change to achieve its stated purposes in today's world. Advocacy may also aim a concerted action at the solution of common problems such as drug abuse, alcoholism, mental retardation, and abuse of civil rights, which affect many families in a community.

Family advocacy service is needed by families at all socioeconomic levels, since it is concerned with provision of a humane social environment for all and is related to problems common to all. Priority for advocacy service should go to families, neighborhoods, and communities in the greatest jeopardy, who have suffered most acutely from the impact of racism, dehumanization, poverty, injustice, and inequality of opportunity.

ADVOCACY: CORE FUNCTION OF A FAMILY SERVICE AGENCY

The family service agency today may offer a wide variety of services: family counseling, family life education, family advocacy, special programs tailored to meet an urgent need of a particular group or community. All are based in the common mission of family service to help people by strengthening the family as the basic institution of human society. Although these various services may be defined and budgeted separately and may call for refinement of different skills to provide the highest competence in each, they should operate in close harmony with each other. There are organic linkages between all service areas, and careful attention to their operation in concert is a necessary element of quality in the total agency program. Any family may benefit from different services at different times or con-current involvement in more than one.

The purpose of this section is to suggest some of the interrelationships of family advocacy and casework, family life education, public issues activity. The intent is not to assign priority for one type of service over another, but to provide board and staff members in family service agencies with concepts that may be useful in policy-making and program-planning adapted specifically to the community in which the individual agency is located. The exact balance among many services and the allocation of resources at a given time will vary appropriately, but FSAA believes that the core program of any family service agency should contain elements of advocacy.

All family service agencies should advocate for the family

as a primary social institution, essential to the healthy development of individuals so that they may function at their maximum capacity in all life's roles and tasks.

All family service agencies should advocate for human rights on the basis of the worth and dignity of every human being of any age, sex, creed, color, or race.

All family service agencies should be clearly committed to the cause of their clients—families—and guard constantly against offering any service that directly or indirectly works against the best interests of families. Agencies should serve people rather than systems.

Casework and advocacy

Family advocacy depends heavily for its knowledge base on casework and other direct-service programs. In turn, a productive family advocacy service will facilitate the effectiveness of casework and other direct services by removing or diminishing external barriers to the achievement of their goals.

Increasingly family service agencies have been asked to serve families with problems and needs beyond the scope of casework service alone. Unless other resources are available when and where they are needed, unless opportunities for high-quality education, health care, employment, housing, and other basic necessities are open to all, unless public policies and private attitudes are geared to provide a just society in which human dignity is valued and preserved, then caseworkers can hope to do little for many clients except help them to endure miserable conditions. Caseworkers have been trained in a theory that the individual has the capacity to change his own condition. Caseworkers understand that an individual may need support and direction as well as faith in the system's ability to help him if he is to negotiate the system's demands. Concerned workers have always struggled to rectify wrongs suffered by individual clients. In individual cases the caseworker is sometimes successful, but this single success does not effect any change in the offending social institution. Eventually the immovability of the bureaucracy will dampen his enthusiasm and he may find himself encouraging the client to come to terms with reality.

CASE TO CAUSE—AND BACK TO CASE

Many, many families in all walks of life can no longer function effectively in a rapidly changing society and the more complicated systems that do not yield to individual negotiation. Growing awareness of impersonality and rigidity in organizations meant to serve people created the case-to-cause—and-back-to-case—aspect of family advocacy.

While the family service agency maintains its responsibility to serve the individual, it becomes also a family advocacy agency when it simultaneously accepts responsibility for trying to change those external forces and conditions that bring people to the agency, affect adversely the ability of many families to function well, lower the quality of family life throughout the community, or bar families from effective use of services intended to help them.

> A helping person and a client coming together on a problem constitute the case. A condition in the community, external to the client, neither caused by him nor subject to his control, is a contributing cause to the problem and a barrier to its resolution. In case to cause Advocacy, the helping person and the client direct corrective attention to the external condition identified as a contributing cause. When that cause is corrected, the helping person and the client can then return to the case, where the client's strengths and the helping person's skills can now be utilized more effectively.[2]

There are a few guidelines that clarify this concept and point up the linkages between casework and advocacy.

> Neither the helping person nor the client necessarily, though they may, participate in the corrective action other than bringing the "cause" to the attention of appropriate persons or organizations and providing testimony or documentation as may be needed. The corrective action has as its goal sys-

tems change, so that the benefit is permanent and affects all future users of that system. The helping process—casework, child placement, legal aid, homemaker or Big Brother service —need not actually come to a halt or recess while the advocacy action is under way.[3]

CASE EXAMPLE

Mrs. A did not appear for her eleven o'clock appointment one morning at family service. She telephoned at 2:30 in the afternoon to explain why. She had had an eight o'clock "appointment" that morning for her four-year-old orthopedically handicapped son at the public child hospital outpatient department. She had arrived promptly at eight with her son, accompanied also by her two-year-old daughter. After standing in line awhile to check in and to identify herself and the nature of her appointment, she was told to have a seat and her name would be called. After perhaps another forty-five minutes, her name was called and she was directed to another section of the hospital where she again checked in and was again told to wait. The wait was even longer here, the children were increasingly restless and uncomfortable, and Mrs. A's eleven o'clock appointment at family service came and went. The children's lunchtime had also come and gone before mother and children completed the purpose of the clinic visit. By the time Mrs. A and the two small children reached home, it was approaching two o'clock, and all three were in a state of near hysteria.

How would most social agencies have responded to this situation, at least during the 1950's and most of the '60's? My guess is that the caseworker, or perhaps a supervisor or administrator of the agency, would have telephoned the Social Service Department of the public hospital, spoken to the medical social worker, a colleague perhaps known personally to the agency social worker, and said something like—For Pete's sake, can't you see that Mrs. A is taken care of on her appointments without her and the children having to wait all day? The medical social worker would have explained the clinic's operating policies and procedures, proving beyond the shadow of a doubt that there was no other way the clinic could function and still get its work done. The medical social worker would find some way, however, to see that Mrs. A got special treatment on her next appointment.

Mrs. A would have an easier experience at the clinic next time and would no longer miss her casework appointments for this reason. The hospital and clinic system would continue to operate in the same way, with hundreds or thousands of other families having experiences similar to that from which Mrs. A is now saved. She was saved by the desire of one social worker to do a favor for a colleague, or perhaps out of respect for the agency, or perhaps because of the wish of a sensitive and sympathetic individual social worker to help another human being. She was not saved because her cause was acknowledged to be just, or because of respect for her rights, her dignity, or her power. There was case-oriented advocacy here, it helped Mrs. A temporarily, and it was accomplished by coupling good intentions with the limited use of power— of individual social workers—a degree of power not possessed by Mrs. A herself.

This hypothetical reconstruction is advanced as a reasonable description of what might have happened before in a typical agency. This same case-to-cause situation was actually handled in this past year by a Family and Children's Agency * with a family advocacy orientation and commitment. First, the caseworker described the problem to the supervisor and Agency administration. Second, the hospital was contacted, in this case by the Family Advocate, though it might have been by an Agency administrative staff member, community worker, or Board member. The hospital confirmed that this was the way they operated, explained their reasons, and agreed to talk further about this matter with representatives of Family Service and other agencies. Third, other agencies were contacted and experience of the effects of this policy documented. Fourth, a meeting was arranged with representatives of agencies and those hospital staff members having the power to modify the systems in question. Fifth, after learning the effects of their policies on the very families they were attempting to help, and being challenged to modify their system in order to serve families better at the relatively low cost of some greater inconvenience to themselves, the

---

* Sunbeam Home and Family Service, Oklahoma City, Oklahoma.

hospital initiated and carried through a thorough revision of its clinic scheduling processes. As a result of the dialogue process, other by-products also came about, including the more effective use of volunteers in the hospital and the way in which the hospital waiting areas were organized and furnished.

The effects of successful advocacy can extend far beyond the precipitating cause. In the case cited above, for instance, the hospital is a teaching center. Fledgling physicians and other trainees were being taught that this type of disregard for the time and dignity of patients is the approved way to operate. Now they are getting a different message which may influence them throughout their careers. The differences between the hypothetical reconstruction and the actual case are both obvious and profound. In the actual case example, there was systems change so that all families affected by the system will benefit both now and continuing into the future. Change came about primarily because of recognition of the manner in which the institution's own policies and practices were defeating their own ends of service to people. The effect of power and the desire to avoid a confrontation or unpleasant incident, or the desire to cooperate or to appear cooperative with community agencies, may also have constituted some part of the motivation for change, but that is irrelevant once the change has come about in the presence of a motivating factor that enhances the stature and functioning of all concerned.[4]

KNOWLEDGE AND SKILLS NEEDED FOR FAMILY ADVOCACY

As in casework, there are six essential parts of the advocacy process: definition of the problem, case study, diagnosis, treatment plan, implementation of the plan, and evaluation.

Whether interviewing a family whose problems are a result of the community or a product of a personal maladjustment, one has to find out the facts.

Whether there are two opposing individuals or a family in opposition to an institution, one must listen to both points of view and determine the direction most likely to bring the opposing views into workable liaison.

Caseworkers need to know the resources . . . when to

seek consultation from a lawyer or a state or city official, as they know when to call in a psychiatrist or refer to another social agency.

Family service personnel need to know how an institution operates just as they need to know how a family system operates.

Family service personnel need to know the other people and agencies working on the problem, so there may be coordination, collaboration, and documentation.

Caseworkers need to work for cooperation, but they cannot refuse to confront if this alternative becomes necessary. Caseworkers know how to use anger, hostility, or resistance to help the client in casework and they can learn to meet the same defenses in institutions and find ways to solve the problem.

Family advocates need to work toward utilizing the highest level of influence and policy-making in an institution—as caseworkers direct their casework skills toward mobilizing the strengths in an individual—in order to remedy the problem.

Family advocates need to bring to bear all that family service agencies know about human behavior, interrelationships, and the mechanisms operating to avoid change in institutions as in individual personality structures. It is necessary to listen and to hear what is really being said, so that an accurate diagnosis of the problem can be made and an effective treatment plan, or strategy for bringing about change, can be found.

CASE EXAMPLE

The Neighborhood Project was initiated to intervene in a slum neighborhood with increasing numbers of school dropouts, high teenage delinquency, increasing illegitimate birth rates among teenage girls, increased use of drugs, and poor family health standards. The area had the second highest juvenile delinquency rate in the city. Over 60 percent of the families living in the neighborhood's public housing project were broken families. School dropouts were considered a serious problem by the area's elementary and junior high schools. Isolated by lack of public transportation, and with poor shopping facilities for low-income families and high transient population, the neighborhood had been identified as a "potential slum" by the Office of Housing and Urban Development. A study made by the family service agency staff member showed that there was a minimum of effective communication among the many community health, welfare, and educational services under city, county, state, and voluntary auspices.

The Child and Family Service of Austin, Texas, recognizing these pressures on families, was successful in securing financial support for the Neighborhood Project from a local family foundation, a foundation interested in mental health, and the Rotary Club. The program was carried out by a project coordinator who was a family agency staff member, and regular meetings of the neighborhood council were held. Subcommittees of the council focused on education and resources, youth activities, housing, and employment. An advisory committee of the family agency board met monthly with the project coordinator. The absence of recreation programs for about twenty-five hundred neighborhood children, a factor in the high delinquency rate, led to the development of an after-school recreation program in cooperation with the parks and recreation department. During the summer months alone, 7,105 children participated in the activities of this program.

There had been no supervised or coordinated programs of informal education and recreation for the 178 families in the housing project. Through the cooperative effort of the housing authority and the city recreation department, sparked by the neighborhood council, a recreation coordinator was hired to develop and organize such programs. Many university and high school volunteers supervised the recreational activities. A study hall and tutoring program for elementary students was initiated and eventually expanded to include junior and senior high school students. Teachers and volunteer tutors worked together to define individual student needs and evaluate progress.

Limited opportunity in the summer elementary school program for upgrading disadvantaged children aroused the interest of the community. Scholarships were set up so that the maximum number of children could attend summer enrichment classes. A summer employment program for teenagers was developed by a group of neighborhood businessmen after personal appeals were made to them. Approximately a hundred teenagers were directed to summer employment.

The family agency advocate assisted the residents in forming a tenants' council to tackle the problems creating poor housing conditions and to promote pride in their home surroundings. The council sponsored clean-up campaigns, secured additional garbage units, playground equipment, lights for public areas, and a section set aside for recreational activities.

Although many problems remained to be solved (among them additional play space for young children; distribution of surplus foods to the elderly; dental care for elementary age schoolchildren; the development of a multiservice center where many organizations could coordinate health and welfare services; and the establishment of a clearing house where employers could secure neighborhood part-time women workers), through meetings of the council, the subcommittees, and the advisory committee and daily contact with the participants have come understanding, recognition of community problems, and a commitment to attack these problems according to approved priority bases.

Family life education and advocacy

Family life education is a term used to cover a wide range of services designed to enrich understanding of interpersonal relationships, to inform participants in such specific areas of family functioning as sex, money management, and child rearing, and to assist family members to widen the boundaries of information and breadth of understanding against which they make choices of behavior in all their life situations. Family life education programs operate under many auspices, and many techniques are used from the mass media to one-to-one instruction. Most often family service agencies offer the small-group discussion method as a most effective way to enhance and facilitate the capacity for social functioning of the family and the individual. These discussions provide material on the external factors affecting family life adversely just as counseling interviews do. A group of people may discover a common external factor that is aggravating the family situations that motivated them to seek family life education, but the individual family may have been unaware, for instance, of a relationship between a school policy and its own rebellious youngster until several parents have reported comparable circumstances in their homes. New information and new understanding should lead to changed attitudes and different behavior. As feelings of isolation and powerlessness are reduced in individual participants, there will often develop a group perception that change may be accomplished through united effort. Many groups will decide to take action together as a group, with staff leadership or the public support of the agency when needed, to fill a gap in community resources, to change a damaging condition in the neighborhood, to bring about a change in policy in schools, agencies, or city hall. Project ENABLE (Project for Education and Neighborhood Action for Better Living Environment) supplied dozens of examples of this kind of "social action." Day-care centers, tutoring programs, recreation areas, and improved housing conditons grew out of ENABLE and similar programs of parent group education.

CASE EXAMPLE

When a family service agency foster mother deplored the fact that the street was the only play space in the neighborhood, a family service graduate student worker assured her that the family service board and staff would act as intermediaries with the city officials if the neighborhood citizens developed a self-help project. Available through the owner, who offered to deed it to the neighborhood, was a 110-foot-square lot filled with broken glass and junk. A group of citizens had tried unsuccessfully to raise money to pay taxes and insurance on it and to equip it. The worker then met several times with the group which incorporated and elected officers. The major project was a rummage and bake sale to secure funds and to arouse the community's interest and support. On the day of the sale there was a large crowd including the city council president, the executive director of the family service agency, and many of the agency's volunteers. The council lauded the efforts of the citizens toward self-improvement of their neighborhood and pledged $1,000 from the city for equipment. The lot was furnished with swings, a jungle gym, seesaws, and benches by city officials who were impressed by the efforts of parents who raised money to pay the back taxes.

This project demonstrates how a student in a family service agency stimulated a previously defeated people to organize and improve their own community. The involvement of the agency, the Family and Children's Society of Baltimore, Maryland, also resulted in recruitment of more foster parents.

An entire group may simultaneously embrace learning objectives and action; or members of the group may be referred to an existing advocacy group concerned with the issue of interest; or the group's original educational focus may be terminated, and a new advocacy group may be formed with staff leadership from the family advocacy department instead of from the family life education staff. Of course, conversely, individuals involved in advocacy activity may wish to become part of a family life education group whose educational focus is likely to be helpful, just as they may at some point be referred to the agency's counseling program when appropriate. Experience in Project ENABLE provided many examples of movement in these directions also.[5]

Public issues: another name for family advocacy?

FSAA membership requirements have long included the statement: "The agency must direct efforts toward the improvement of social conditions that have a negative effect on family life." [6] To implement this goal, there has often been a public issues committee charged to "assist the board, the executive director, and other staff members in fulfilling the agency's second major function—improving the social environment. It recommends policy on public issues and directs efforts toward improving social conditions, on the local, state, and national levels." [7]

There is clearly a direct relationship between these statements that go back to the earliest tradition of family service and everything that has been written and said about family advocacy. What is new is the focus on systems change and a growing body of knowledge of theory and technique. FSAA is proud that family advocacy is not totally new but encompasses the best of family service and social work goals and values over the years.

Under the name of public issues, family service agencies have often taken positions or written letters to congressmen, but sometimes without effective follow-up or direct involvement in issues at a local level where the people live whose private pain creates the public issues. Family service agencies are in a position not only to recognize that great social problems are made up of very personal agonies, but to take a leading role in making the community, the state, and the nation aware of the facts and helping those in power to understand and respond constructively to the needs of people.

Public issues as practiced in the past might be more accurately termed *legislative action,* often limited not only by inadequate resources of political skills and staff time but also by concern for laws and policies governing the tax-exempt organization's right to "influence" legislators. This aspect of advocacy will be discussed later. It is sufficient here to say that family advocacy service should have a much broader goal than legislative action and, in that sense, includes but is not restricted to a traditional concept of public issues.

CASE EXAMPLE
Family Service Association of Nassau County, New York, had a call from a widow with two children, whose income was a social security check supplemented by public assistance. The landlord had recently raised the rent considerably above the amount provided by the Department of Public Welfare, and the women was one month behind on her rent and was threatened with eviction. Because one child was seriously handicapped and because there was an acute housing shortage, it was imperative to keep the family in the present apartment. If evicted, the only accommodation the Department of Public Welfare could find for the family was in a motel at $1,200 per month. The family advocate became involved and arranged to pay one month's rent, pending a protest on the restrictive public assistance regulations.

The family social worker acting as an advocate then called a meeting of fourteen family and other voluntary agencies to compare experiences and to obtain case illustrations to use in further efforts. The material collected was widely distributed among churches, health and welfare agencies, service clubs, and business groups. The family advocate made a number of speeches—one helped set off a hunger march by Lutheran churches. This netted $20,000 of which half was entrusted to the family service agency to administer for welfare crises. A conference was set up with a key state legislator, two family agency clients, and the advocate, and another agency's client and staff member. This helped the legislator push for some state welfare changes which did materialize, although they were not entirely adequate.

A thorough study of the state law and regulations was made, together with a review of pending and settled court

cases at various levels. With this as a base, a coalition committee of agencies was convened. The committee held
regular meetings with Department of Public Welfare officials
and gained a number of improvements in relation to the flat
grant system, and the separation of income maintenance and
social services.

Quality factors of family advocacy service

A task force on standards recommended some guidelines for
services in a family service agency to the standards development committee of FSAA recently. Among other things, the
task force listed certain "quality factors" that would be
present in the model family advocacy service program:

1. All staff members must share an obligation to promote
advocacy service, to use advocacy methods as appropriate in
their own service roles, and to provide clients with opportunities to work with advocacy groups, as indicated. (See
the subsequent discussion, "Who Are the Family Advocates?")

2. The case evaluation and interviewing methods of social
workers in a family counseling program must include significant attention to the dysfunctional aspects of social institutions and conditions as they affect the family situation, as
well as the traditional and necessary attention to the pathology and dysfunctional aspects within the family and its
members. The counselors must be able to distinguish the
ways in which factors in both these areas are affecting their
families' life situations and be able to initiate social work
intervention in relating to both. (See the discussion of interviewing for family advocacy in "Family Advocacy: from Case
to Cause," in Part 3.) Similarly, staff members who work in
family life education programs must be able to identify the
point at which members of a group see a necessity for action
in regard to a common problem and to assist them or refer
them to an advocacy program.

3. Accumulated evidence from review of the total service

load in all program areas such as family counseling and family life education must be sought and collected as the source of family service knowledge about institutional dysfunction. This information should be used to suggest new objectives or new perceptions in the advocacy program.

Evaluation

In a complicated and developing helping method, evaluation in terms of success or failure may be difficult. An agency may fight hard to defeat a certain piece of legislation and the bill may still pass. Certainly the agency has failed in its ultimate objective, but if the community is now truly alive to the issue, if many people are now alert to potential damage to the quality of life for themselves or their fellow citizens, if the agency and others in the community are now mobilized to start new approaches to eliminate a perceived threat, then has not the agency rendered an effective service to the families of its community? On the other hand, the agency may succeed and the bill may be defeated but a dozen other groups, most of the local media, and a leading politican or two were all in the struggle somewhere. Who gets credit? What really did the job? Did the agency's effort really make any difference and was it worth the time involved?

In achieving a reformed welfare system, in getting passage or defeat of an important piece of legislation, in improving a disintegrating public education system, many groups must play crucial roles. The climate of the times, the personalities and interests of civic leaders, and accidents of history will contribute to success or failure. Difficulties of evaluation, reporting, and assigning proper credit (or blame) cannot deter an agency from undertaking an advocacy program nor prevent it from applying its aggregate knowledge and skill to development and implementation of a high-quality professional advocacy service for its community. There is no substitute for thoughtful planning and flexible structuring. (Member agencies should find a 1971 publication of FSAA,

The Accreditation Process of FSAA, a very useful tool, readily adaptable to the needs of evaluating an advocacy program.)

In evaluating any professional service of the agency, it is necessary first to have clearly enunciated goals for the program set down by the board. Priorities must then be established in relation to conditions in its own community including resources of expertise, time, and potential impact available to the agency. Priorities need to be reexamined frequently as new information and experience accumulate. Each advocacy action undertaken should have its own objectives realistically spelled out and related to the agency's goals and priorities.

Evaluation of advocacy service, like evaluation of any agency program, must include feedback from the people most directly affected—those families served. Many mistakes can be avoided by involving consumers of service in the process from the beginning—at the point of deciding to become an advocacy agency—and then in determining goals, priorities, and objectives.

Further suggestions on evaluation and reporting of an advocacy program will be given at the end of Part 1.

GUIDELINES FOR DEVELOPING A FAMILY ADVOCACY PROGRAM

Internal advocacy

Inspired by a progressive board, imaginative executive, future-oriented staff, client demands, or community pressure, an agency has decided it must move into advocacy. How to begin?

DESIRABLE BASIC CONDITIONS
It is helpful to have some experience in advocacy functioning without necessarily having labeled it such. The agency builds

credibility for its advocacy role by demonstration. The most urgent place to begin is within the agency itself. One's own house should be in order first. This phase of advocacy program development is called internal advocacy.

It is necessary to build a durable commitment, one that will not fade away in the face of controversial issues, a budget squeeze, mistakes and failures, an ungrateful community. This commitment does not mean that every single board and staff member has to be totally convinced; most people learn from experience, and for some people myths aren't laid to rest until they have personally lived through something that dispels them.

EARLY STEPS

From the experience of the many family service agencies deeply involved in developing an advocacy program, it is possible to describe some of the steps an agency can take, without the expenditure of any great amount of money.

A joint committee of board and staff members is appointed. It may be called a task force, a study group, an ad hoc committee. Its charge is to consider the full implications for the agency, the community, and, most important, for the families who are present and potential clients of the agency, of a comprehensive family advocacy service.

The committee will arrive at some conclusions and make recommendations perhaps to the public issues committee, the executive committee, or to the full board.

CASE EXAMPLE

A report first stated its charge and named committee members. Consultants with special interest and knowledge were invited to attend meetings. Three board members and three staff members attended a workshop on family advocacy held in their region and led by FSAA "faculty." The report then defined family advocacy and stated a conviction that the adoption of this concept is essential to achievement of basic agency goals. The report stated in addition:

This does not mean that the "pure counseling" approach emphasized in the past is outdated or that it is now being replaced by something else. Family advocacy merely offers our agency and its staff an additional technique for helping clients and their families.

It is the belief of this committee that family advocacy will complement the "pure counseling" approach and offer the agency and its staff an additional method to overcome time-consuming and repetitive efforts that have been ineffective and unsuccessful in the past in solving basic problems facing those who come to us for assistance.

We realize that while the family advocacy approach may appear to be new, it has been part of the operation of this agency in the past.[8]

The report continued by citing past or current agency programs involving advocacy functioning and concluded with the recommendations that the agency "formally accept the concept of family advocacy as part of its operating procedure" and "that a family advocacy committee be established and this committee suggest and recommend ways in which it should function."

NEXT STEPS

A permanent family advocacy committee is responsible for promoting, establishing, and maintaining agency commitment. One way to begin is with a reeducation process that may include an agency workshop, several study groups or fact-finding task forces, and seminars led by specialists.[9]

Among the questions and issues that may be considered are:

Board and staff constituency

Is the agency really representative of the community? How are board members selected? How does the agency receive information on needs and problems of all families in the community? Does the agency plan with people, not just for them, and is it sufficiently representative of groups to be served to make planning with them possible?

Agency program

Has the agency looked at its open caseload and cases closed in recent years to see what clusters of problems may be identified or to evaluate the success of treatment methods, and the relationships between diagnosis and presumed outcome? Are outpost offices, detached workers, special projects, outreach programs connected with the agency so that there is easy flow of information and service from one to another?

Agency policies and procedures

What is the agency doing to make itself part of the solution rather than part of the problem? Are staff members located where people who need them can find them? Are offices open when people can keep appointments—or drop in when need is urgent? What are the agency's attitudes toward poor people, minority groups, old people, hippies, students with long hair, communes, unconventional families? What are the agency's attitudes about abortion, interracial adoption, confrontation, family planning, women's lib? Is the agency able to refute myths with facts about such groups and issues? Is the agency keenly aware that attitudes are often more eloquently reflected by the behavior of receptionists, volunteers, secretaries, executives, board officers, and professional staff members than by position statements? Is commitment limited to office hours and meetings of the board, or does everyone associated with the agency speak and act for people's rights and a just society in his life away from the agency—in suburbia; at his club, Parent-Teachers Association meetings, church, dinner parties; in meetings of other groups; in his own family?

SOME RISKS IN INTERNAL ADVOCACY

Internal advocacy is a tough, painful, self-involved process. It is basic and essential to an effective family advocacy service program, but it carries its own risks. An agency can get so caught up in self-study and self-blame that it never gets around to action to change anything. It can become so overwhelmed by the size and complexity of newly discovered problems that it cannot decide where to start or whether it really has the power or skill to make any difference. There is power in social work and social agencies. It must be used judiciously and not thrown around nor allowed to lie fallow.

Another possible risk in internal advocacy comes from a need to have everything perfect before moving into external advocacy: unanimous commitment, adequate funds, expert staff, answers for every possible contingency. An agency could hide behind an intensive self-study, prolonged research for the "right" information and techniques, careful consideration of all the risks. It could simultaneously soothe itself that it is facing up to the problem, recognizing its own weaknesses and limitations, and yet stay comfortably in its traditional niche with the hope that others will eliminate the necessity for any serious change or controversial action by the agency.

Perhaps the most important risk to consider is the risk in *not* changing. If a family service agency cannot get on the side of making systems work for all families and does not put words and commitment into action, it must abandon the field to those who do have conviction and courage to try. Practically speaking, this may well increase competition for limited funds from more relevant groups and helping methods devised in response to today's consumer demand. A body of knowledge developed through decades of experience can be lost to society if a family service agency fails to understand that, as in every other field, there is much more to be learned and yesterday's answers may not fit today's questions. To hold fast to today's system will mean to be lost—or even dead—tomorrow.

External advocacy

INTERVIEWING FOR FAMILY ADVOCACY
There is a tendency for the family caseworker to focus his attention on the individual or family dysfunction, in the

interview, rather than turning his attention to the institution which may be a factor in producing this pathology. Interviewing for advocacy introduces new factors into the sessions with the client and with public and private organizations on behalf of the client. On occasion, an assessment of pathology in a client may distort the caseworker's evaluation of an injustice, or value judgments of the client's mismanagement of some area of his life may cause the caseworker to react unfavorably to the client, and thus fail to develop the commitment necessary for advocacy for the client. An important step in advocacy is a commitment to the client rather than to the existing system.[10]

SETTING PRIORITIES

Cases for advocacy may come from several sources: agency caseloads in both individual and group services, local newspapers, experience or information of an individual board or staff member derived from their various capacities in other community service organizations, at work or at home in their own neighborhoods.

Those family service agencies serving a large number of families through a diversified program reaching many sections of the community and many kinds of families may not wish or need to go beyond the issues concerning the families in the agency's current caseload. Some agencies may, however, decide to begin with an issue brought to their attention from another source if they become convinced that the situation must be adversely affecting families including clients. It seems likely that when an agency's concern for this cause becomes known, some clients may well feel able to discuss their experience with the situation and relate it to the problems that brought them to the agency.

It cannot be stated too often that the immediate objectives and priorities for an advocacy program should be individualized by each agency, just as the objectives and plan for the casework treatment of an individual family are related to that specific situation.

Priorities will vary for many reasons. Agencies under sectarian or ethnic auspices will often give first priority to sectarian or ethnic concerns. Agencies in large cities may feel that certain causes have great urgency while agencies in smaller communities may find their priorities fall into another order.

Jewish family agencies have a long and rich history of advocacy in combatting discrimination, and meeting the needs of the aging and alienated youth. Their experience must be valuable to the whole field as techniques and methods are refined.

An example of advocacy as practiced by the Jewish Family Service of Philadelphia (JFS) is evidenced in the following testimony presented by the agency at the Urban Coalition Hearing in Philadelphia on December 2, 1971.

> The Jewish Family Service of Philadelphia wishes to thank you for the invitation to be present today and considers it a privilege to be included among those agencies invited to present their views at this public hearing. In order to place our comments within an appropriate context, permit me to first speak briefly about our agency. The Jewish Family Service, which is now in its 103rd year of operation, is a voluntary agency which has a program of services for persons of all ages to help resolve problems that may arise in their day-to-day living. Thirty-five percent of our agency clientele is over age sixty, and of this 35 percent, 90 percent are living on marginal or submarginal incomes. Social Security, Old Age Assistance, and pensions are their three major sources of incomes. Recognizing the increasing problems of inadequate delivery of health care services and further recognizing that 11 percent of the Philadelphia population are over age sixty-five and that of this number only 5 percent live in institutions, it is in behalf of the aged living in their own homes that we wish to speak.
>
> Unfortunately, we do not see answers to this enormously complicated and perplexing problem, nor is this within our area of expertise. However, we feel tremendous obligation to

Reprinted from *Social Casework*, June 1972.

present some facts and to highlight the tragedies that come from our present grossly inadequate system of delivery of health care services.

Too well we know that frequency of illness increases with age and that studies have established the fact that 86 percent of those over age sixty-five have one or more chronic diseases. Jewish Family Service sees as one of its major functions to help with the problems that are created by ill health and to help our older clients secure the appropriate care and attention needed to enable them to continue to live in their own homes as healthily and happily as possible.

Given these problems, there are certain consequences which inevitably arise to which we wish to address ourselves.

1. How can the health care system adequately provide services to those having restricted mobility, acute health crises, shortage of finances, long-term chronic illness—all these with their numerous accompanying adjuncts?

A case in point is that of Mr. H, age eighty-three, who has a malignancy of the bladder and wears a colostomy bag. Arteriosclerosis has resulted in chronic brain damage, and he is now confined to bed. He needs help with feeding, being kept clean, as well as tending to numerous other physical needs. His wife, Mrs. H, in her early eighties, has chronic heart failure and is exhausting herself trying to continue to care for him. Two married children are constantly running to the house after their working hours to help in whatever way they can. Savings have been exhausted, and although the Hs have qualified for nursing home care, no nursing home will admit Mr. H because the Department of Public Assistance grant is their only source of income. Until some more satisfactory plan can be worked out, such as admission to a nursing home, Jewish Family Service is providing the services of a housekeeper, realizing in this situation this is really not the helpful solution. How does the health care system see itself meeting the needs of the many Mr. and Mrs. Hs who are living in our community?

2. How does the health care system see itself providing alternatives to the single most expensive medical care system in the world, namely, the private practitioner-patient system?

We recently received a call from concerned neighbors in the community to inform us that a former stroke patient, age seventy-six, was ill and could not leave her home for necessary medical attention. Our social worker, who, within a few hours, visited in response to the community's concern, found Mrs. L to be an alert elderly woman who had not had decent medical care in almost a year. She could not walk down the flight of stairs nor use transportation to the nearby hospital clinic, and numerous calls to the physicians in the neighborhood had brought the response of "no house calls." How does the health care system see itself providing for the many Mrs. Ls in our community who need medical care right within their own homes?

3. How does the health care system see itself solving the problem of providing maintenance medications (1) to those aged who live on inadequate incomes (35 percent of the elderly have incomes below the established poverty level) and cannot afford to purchase drugs and (2) for those who have slightly higher incomes where the sale of such drugs is on a maximized profit basis?

Another case in point is that of Mr. T, a retired salesman in his late seventies, who has a combined income from Social Security and pension amounting to $193 a month. His rent is $90 a month excluding utilities. He is a diabetic and also suffers from chronic congestive heart failure. His bills for medicine average at least $25 to $30 monthly. After his rent and utilities are paid, he has $80 monthly left for food, clothing, and medication. His choices are tragic—if he purchases the necessary medicine, he has no money left for food. Should he medicate himself properly and literally starve? Shall he neglect his medication and go into diabetic shock?

How can the delivery of health care services be modified effectively to meet the needs of the hundreds of thousands of Mr. Ts living in our communities today?

These problems are only a few of those we encounter in our day-to-day practice. The answers to these questions must come from the urgent revision of state and federal legislation relative to our health service system. It is their social responsibility. The lack of available resources and services in the community and the lack of coordination among health and welfare resources and personnel have been compounded over the last decade. Even within the limitations of the Jewish Family Service program of services, our experience has demonstrated dramatically the inestimable value of helping many chronically ill older persons to continue to live in their own homes. In human terms it has tremendous meaning to the older person and his family and, in terms of dollars and cents, is far less costly than a hospital or nursing home bed. In the year 1970, we provided service to 1,642 older clients.

Through our program of supportive services, such as homemakers, housekeeping services, use of Friendly Visitors, shopping services, and counseling services offered by our social work staff, we were able to help older persons to continue to live independently in their own homes. In this respect, we are both a deliverer and a seeker of health services—both the provider and consumer. As consumers, in our role as enablers, we are often the mechanism of communication between the resource (if it exists) and the client. As experienced seekers of health services for our clients, we speak to the lack of availability, accessibility, and accountability, as well as to the lack of coordination, communication, and concern. The problem is a gigantic and an enormous one, to be sure. Only through improved and creative state and federal legislation which calls for significant and drastic changes in our current systems of health can effective planning and delivery of health services to meet overall community needs be achieved. Hopefully, such an improved health delivery system would respect the rights and dignity of both the providers and the recipients of health services. The Philadelphia Urban Coalition is to be highly commended for taking steps in this direction in lending its efforts to fulfilling our social responsibility to the many Mr. and Mrs. Hs, the Mrs. Ls, and the Mr. Ts who reside in our communities.

CASE EXAMPLE

Counseling of minors without the consent of their parents has been for many years a difficult problem that has troubled not only family service agencies, but psychiatric hospitals, child guidance clinics, and mental health clinics, as well as private physicians who have been asked from time to time to provide treatment for their underage patients without the knowledge of their parents.

In 1970, Jewish Family Service began its Project on Troubled Youth in the western suburbs of Philadelphia. In order to reach these adolescents, they were assured that the agency would not get in touch with their parents without their consent. Simultaneously, the agency was engaged in running "rap sessions" in its northwest district office where the same ground rules were used. While it was felt certain that this was the best way to proceed in order to involve the youth on a free-choice basis, the agency was advised by legal counsel that there were a number of risks involved in such practice. The only thing that provided reassurance for the agency was counsel's opinion that, as long as it eventually intended to involve the parents, it did not run a great risk of jeopardy. However, the problem still remained a troubling one because of the legal aspects.

The issue was formally brought to the public issues committee for attempted resolution. The agency called upon the consultative and library resources of the Family Service Association of America. All the collected data indicated that no member agency of FSAA had any assurance that it would have any protection of any sort if difficulties arose.

The public issues committee, following study of the issue, recommended to the board of directors that the agency attempt to get immunity legislation passed by the state legislature. By using the resources of Community Services of Pennsylvania, a voluntary, statewide, citizens' advisory agency, and the knowledge and interest of several of the board and committee members, the committee canvassed the available legislation, both existing and proposed, to see if there was any way for the agency to have either a bill or an amendment on existing legislation enacted.

The chairman of the advisory committee, a young, politically knowledgeable attorney, provided the political expertise necessary. The consensus of the public issues committee, after a review of existing and proposed legislation, was that it would be more practical to seek an amendment to some proposed legislation than to try to get a bill offered de novo in the legislature.

A bill was selected that was being offered in the state senate to provide immunity to physicians treating youths with drug problems. This bill was seen as having the greatest likelihood of success because of the political influence of physicians and the fact that the bill, if enacted, would not cost the taxpayers of Pennsylvania any money. Although the bill had many legislative sponsors, the agency was fortunate that one of them was a state senator from Philadelphia, and this was one of the reasons why the bill was chosen. Contact was made with this senator, through the good offices of one of the members of the JFS board of directors, who was of the same political persuasion as the senator, and who had considerable behind-the-scenes political influence within the city. The senator was invited to a meeting of the public issues committee, at which time the agency's proposed amendment, allowing accredited family service agencies of Pennsylvania to counsel adolescents, was introduced. The senator was agreeable, providing the medical society had no objections to an amendment being tacked on to a bill which was originally offered on their behalf. JFS undertook the responsibility of clearing this with the local medical society, which sent a letter to the chairman of the Committee on Public Health and Welfare indicating their support of the amendment. It was also cleared with the general director of FSAA.

At the same time, the public issues committee involved the twenty-two member agencies of FSAA in the state of Pennsylvania to enlist their support in writing to their state senators and representatives on behalf of State Senate Bill No. 1034 which was being offered in the senate. JFS also provided the senator with copies of the agency's hundred-year history as well as material about FSAA, including its concerns about standards and accreditation. The senator had requested this as background information in order to reassure himself—and legitimately so—that the agency and its accrediting bodies were not "fly-by-night outfits."

When next the agency heard from the senator, State Senate Bill No. 1034 had been incorporated into House Bill No. 850 which was part of a comprehensive drug bill which reevaluated all the state's involvement with drug usage, changing several laws and modifying others. Most important for family service agencies was one section allowing agencies and clinics "to offer counseling to youth who were involved in drugs without the obligation of involving the parents, if this was counter-indicated by either the youth's wishes or because of treatment considerations." The bill was signed into law in May 1972, by Governor Shapp.

The senator was honored at the agency's May 25, 1972, board meeting and public tribute was paid to him for his leadership and guidance in providing what is now the first legislation in the country that provides immunity to counseling agencies. The senator was sufficiently impressed with the outpouring of gratitude and recognition that came from the board to spontaneously offer five state senatorial scholarships for students whom the agency would designate, as well as a senatorial commendation for the efforts and achievements of the JFS in serving youth and in strengthening family life.

This, in effect, represents the summation of over two year's concentrated work in the political arena, to provide immunity legislation for family service agencies.

DIFFERENT PRIORITIES, THE SAME GOAL
Priorities will differ though the goal of family advocacy is universal: to achieve a better quality of life for all families.

The family advocacy committee should have responsibility for (1) selecting issues appropriate for agency action; (2) assigning some priority in relation to resources, urgency, and need; and (3) developing a plan of action that should include delegation of responsibilities for implementation to individuals and other groups (a specific department or subcommittee) within the agency.

A dilemma is posed in the assessment of priorities and allocation of resources. If limits are not set, staff can quickly become over-committed with resultant confusion and inadequate follow-through on tasks. On the other hand, setting of limits can result in too rigid and narrow a focus, without the flexibility to move in quickly on unanticipated opportunities for intervention.

Another dilemma arises between the delegation of authority to the Family Advocate and his accountability to the Board of Directors. Too much delegation leaves the Board helpless and possibly committed to indefensible actions; too much accountability can hamstring the program and make the Advocate into a messenger between the Board and other groups. Workable balances can result from careful policy setting at various levels, from administrative participation, and from review of actions.

The influence of the Family Advocate program depends also upon painstaking data collection, upon careful study of laws and regulations, upon familiarity with past and present moves and controversies. We have found that these gain the respect and ear of legislators and political and other leaders. They tend to be unmoved by oft-repeated general arguments couched in appeals to fairness, humaneness, etc., unless backed up by assembled and clarified data they can rely upon. While this may be outside the usual area of functioning for social workers, it is the vital groundwork for advocacy efforts.[11]

CAUSES GROWING OUT OF CASES

When examination of agency caseload reveals cases for advocacy, they may appear on the surface to be isolated instances. It is not necessary, however, to wait for more examples to appear at the agency when common sense and normal judgment suggest that other people unknown to the agency must be similarly oppressed—remember the example of the mother waiting at the clinic most of the day. The caseworker who encounters firsthand a case for advocacy needs to familiarize himself with the institutions involved and the legal implications, as well as the specific client, problem, and situation. Whether the client seeks help for a problem in which rights are apparently being violated or for some other difficulty in which an advocacy need is implicit, the caseworker should regard the problem as one which the client and the social institution possibly share, and the solution to which may lie outside the client. Where possible legal rights are involved, the caseworker needs some knowledge of the law and a working relationship with a legal service or lawyer who handles advocacy cases. He must, in addition, be prepared to present to the client the difficulties involved in pursuing a court case and the possible alternative solutions. The caseworker as advocate needs a knowledge of other areas as well. The violation of rights other than legal rights may require on the part of the caseworker a familiarity with school policies, credit practices, psychiatric facilities, probationary methods, and so on. The caseworker must be familiar with the hierarchy of command of each important organization in the community, in order to know to whom grievances should first be addressed, what further steps are possible, and the possible methods of retaliation against the client, for the institution must be regarded as an adversary rather than as a cooperating agency, though the reverse may be true in some cases.[12]

CASE EXAMPLE
Acute lead poisoning was the cause of the second hospital admission in two years of a three-year-old boy. The city health department had been called immediately after the child's first admission; a check was made of the apartment where he lived with his mother and two brothers. The building was so saturated with lead paint that there seemed to be no way of removing all traces without tearing it down.

The pediatrician who called Family Counseling of Greater New Haven, Connecticut, stated that he could not release the child from the hospital a second time without assurance that a safe, lead-free apartment was available. "If we get that child a third time, he'll be either seriously brain damaged or dead," the social worker was told.

Efforts were made by the agency to locate an apartment in a housing project. It was well known that one of the top administrators in the housing authority had serious personal objections to providing housing to unwed mothers. The agency talked to the housing authority protesting the rigid "policy," with a follow-up letter to the mayor. Within two days the mother and her three boys were rehoused.

The family service agency, the hospital where the child had been confined, and several other agencies began discussions with the city health department and the housing authority about the whole problem of lead poisoning. An organization, Citizens Against Lead, was formed to alert the community to the dangers of lead poisoning and to work with the housing authority and the redevelopment agency to eliminate lead-based paint from existing housing. A bill was introduced in the state legislature to prohibit the use of all lead-based paint from housing construction and renovation in the state and to label all paint sold according to lead content.

The family service agency supported the bill through letters from board and staff and through testimony at legislative hearings, citing illustrations of families endangered by lead poisoning. The bill was passed during a subsequent session of the general assembly.

CASE EXAMPLE

Agencies that offer foster care for children and an adoption service often find that there are a few children who stay in long-term foster care because they are hard to place in adoption homes. Often these children become very much a part of the foster family, but they are denied the security of adoption because the foster family is unable to assume full economic responsibility.

The advocate in one agency became concerned about a child whose medical expenses were heavy but whose foster family loved him and considered him their own.[13] However, there was no way to assure him the care he needed from their limited income. The advocate began to investigate the possibility of a subsidized adoption. He learned that fourteen states have laws permitting such arrangements, and he wrote to each of these state departments of public welfare requesting information about their law, the number of children permanently placed in this way, an estimate of savings to the state, and any problems arising from application of the law. Meanwhile he learned that personnel in his own state department of welfare were not unfavorable to a subsidized adoption law but considered it "politically unfeasible." They were cooperative in documenting the need throughout the state. Other child-placing agencies throughout the state were queried and were quick to give support to the concept. A state representative willing to introduce a bill was located.

Throughout this period, the advocate had discussed the situation at each monthly meeting of the agency's public issues committee. Armed with supportive information from other states and the interest of other voluntary agencies, he was able to secure their active support. A presentation to the state advisory committee of the department of public welfare resulted in a resolution in support of subsidized adoption that was given good publicity in the morning newspaper.

The state representative referred the advocate and a board member to the legislative council for advice on drafting a bill. The state representative also referred them to a state senator who agreed to sponsor a companion bill. The advocate collected a number of cosponsors and obtained the support of the commissioner of finance, the commissioner of welfare, the welfare department's legal department, and the legal council to insure a sound introduction for the bill in time for action during the legislative session. The other member agencies of FSAA in the state helped in generating statewide support and the bill passed in both houses unanimously.

CAUSES COMING FROM OUTSIDE AGENCY CASELOAD

Things happening in the community may propel the agency to move into more extensive advocacy. A school strike, racial clashes, welfare cuts, an outbreak of deaths from drug abuse, a rise in the number of pregnant schoolgirls, many other symptoms of a troubled community may not be immediately reflected in the agency's caseload but cannot be ignored by a community agency committed to serve families.

The family advocacy committee should keep informed

about all such developments and help the agency decide where, when, and how to intervene. Again, fact-gathering is usually the first step. The agency needs to know who is affected, what it is costing the community (in dollars, wherever possible, as well as in psychological damage, loss of prestige and self-respect, tension, fear, and family disruption), who or what is primarily responsible, who else in the community is concerned, who is opposed to any action, what efforts have been made to remedy the problem, why they did not succeed. In casework, the worker, with or without consultation with other staff, selects the methods and modes of treatment for each client, based on case evaluation. In family advocacy, similar steps are indicated from initial awareness of a problem through a study of the situation and diagnostic thinking about causes and effects to the selection of interventions.

STRATEGIES TO CONSIDER

Because the selection of which interventions to use is a complex one, expert consultation is desirable in an ongoing advocacy program. The wide range of possible interventions includes surveys and studies, which form the groundwork for further action; conferences with other agencies; such educational methods as pamphlets, panels, and press coverage; the official taking of a position; grievance procedures through an ombudsman or other forms of administrative redress; direct approach to officials; petitions; demonstrations; and ad hoc groupings of organizations, or client groups, for a specific objective.[14]

WHO ARE THE FAMILY ADVOCATES?

Special staffing or allocation of staff time to the advocacy program will vary according to agency size and funding, capacities of personnel, and community factors.

Experience among FSAA member agencies suggests that the most effective advocacy programs develop teams of board members, executives, professional staff, paraprofessional staff, and, as appropriate, community people most immediately affected by the problem. Specialists in particular service or problem areas (education, housing, labor laws, credit) are identified and available, either as volunteers or with pay.

The Family Advocate program cannot function properly as a traditional "department." Its staff needs quick access to administration and key Board people for spot conferences, for brainstorming sessions, for decisions. Priorities may have to be reassessed immediately and allocation of time shifted. Such meetings also produce the cross-fertilization of ideas and the pooling of thinking for decision-making which lead to soundness, conviction, and depth in each undertaking.

The Family Advocate cannot function alone. Back-up staff is essential; most community issues tend to develop related or subsidiary problems which may require immediate handling. Or, efforts may have to be projected over a fairly long period of time. Either way, the Advocate cannot maintain flexibility without back-up staff to fill in on specific tasks. In this way also, diffusion of the program through the agency is facilitated and the danger of an isolated program is reduced.[15]

Agency board

Most boards delegate responsibility for family advocacy to a committee. Many agencies have a public issues committee in existence. Such a committee may assume responsibility for overseeing the agency's advocacy program. A new committee should be established, however, if the public issues committee is focused only on legislation—bills actually introduced into local, state, or federal legislative bodies—and is not prepared to take action on issues arising from local conditions, injustices, and hardships arising from the implementation of existing legislation, on education of the community, service gaps, or new legislative needs. The public issues committee may then (1) remain a specialized group whose information and expertise should always be available when appropriate to the advocacy committee (and vice versa); (2) become a subcommittee of advocacy, taking direction in its activity from the priorities established by the advocacy program; or (3) be discontinued as a group with individual members accepting assignment to the advocacy committee or its ad hoc task forces according to their special interests and expertise. Most advocacy activity falls into one of a few major categories, each with its own legislative concerns and its own need for specialized information on housing, transportation, health, welfare, education, employment and training, and interpersonal or intrafamilial matters such as divorce, family planning, drug abuse, day care, delinquency, and so on. Many of the latter are of course related directly and indirectly to one or more of the other categories.

The board through the channel of the advocacy committee is responsible first for the agency's commitment to advocacy. The board must be informed about the concepts and rationale of advocacy and the problems and issues of the community, set up a workable structure involving the whole agency—staff, board, and volunteers—in an ongoing activity, establish priorities, maintain close and continuing contact with the staff, and become jointly or individually involved in action.

The board will then take these steps:

1. Participate actively and intensively in internal advocacy processes

2. See to it that an appropriate amount of time is allocated to advocacy, including a reasonable proportion of the time spent on staff development

3. Study the methods, successes, and failures of the advocacy program and develop guidelines for future efforts

4. Protect clients from letdown because the agency has promised action and then abandons the cause if it gets tough, is controversial, provokes attack, or because staff changes, budget problems, or new enthusiasms distract attention

5. Give careful thought to risks for the agency, help select strategies promising the best return, deal honestly with those who have asked for help that the agency cannot or will not give, follow through once started

6. Attend public meetings and hearings and testify when appropriate, call upon officials and legislators, mobilize influential people not affiliated with the agency

7. Give of individual, specialized knowledge and skill in such areas as law, education, public relations, medicine, and business

8. Advocate for the agency with the United Way and other funding sources, and be prepared to interpret the program, validate agency involvement, relate advocacy to the purposes and goals of the funding body as well as of the Agency

The board of directors may be split to some degree, and votes will no longer be unanimous. Experience indicates, however, that the board can become more vital rather than less so, and that in many advocacy situations board members are themselves the most effective advocates. Without their understanding of the issues and awareness of client problems, the agency will often find its effectiveness reduced and the quality of its professional service diminished.

CASE EXAMPLE

At one advocacy workshop, a board president who had been on the board for many years said that until advocacy came along, she had found her satisfaction from the prestige of affiliation with the "best," most professional agency in town. She had faith in the somewhat mysterious skills of the staff, accepted the sacred concept of confidentiality, and contented herself with being a good board member, always supporting the agency executive who clearly knew what was best for the agency and thus the community. Now —with an advocacy program that demands not her benign approval but her active involvement in learning how people are living in her city, their feelings and needs, and in using her own network of relationships to help bring about the necessary changes—she feels really useful, an important part of the team.[16]

Executive director

Ideally, the executive director is chief advocate in any agency. He is responsible to the board for seeing that the agency serves its clients well. When the board commits the agency to an advocacy service, the executive director is then responsible for providing a high-quality service. If the agency employs a specialist to coordinate advocacy activity, he must be thought of as an assistant to the director and must work closely with him and with the board.

The executive director must be an active member of the advocacy committee and should exercise his leadership and management skills in establishing the agency's advocacy structure, promoting the internal advocacy process, maintaining both board and staff involvement in advocacy activity.

The executive director must feel himself to be a full-time advocate—for the family and for the agency's clients. He will not permit himself to be an agent of depersonalized systems nor a purveyor of poor services.

The executive director will act as an advocate personally by attending public meetings and hearings, testifying when appropriate; mobilizing other executives of agencies and organizations serving people who are victims of adverse conditions; supporting the staff and encouraging the board; carrying out his professional commitment to families in his behavior and by his words in his private life as well as in his office.

Director of professional services

The person carrying the title of director of professional services (DPS), or carrying these responsibilities under any other title in an agency committed to an advocacy program, must first understand and accept the concept that family advocacy is a professional service with a body of knowledge, principles, and methods already in existence and being rapidly but soundly expanded.

The DPS will have a vital role in integrating advocacy service within the total agency functioning. He will recognize and exemplify the professional obligation (not option) of any social worker for social action, for carrying through to the finish for clients' rights and needs.

The DPS is usually responsible for the agency's staff development program and will utilize this function to plan and implement advocacy training for all staff, with or without the M.S.W. degree. He will make certain that he himself is knowledgeable in the principles and methods of advocacy and particularly that he understands and facilitates the linkages to other programs and the application of casework skills and knowledge.

In his supervisory role he can help staff members develop their interviewing skills for advocacy. He can also help all staff members be alert to the many seemingly minor harassments and petty indignities to which clients are subjected and recognize how these may lead some individuals to come to believe that they deserve the situation in which they find themselves. He can help staff understand that when there is a difference between the agency and the client or the client group in perception of where the problem is, it is often good advocacy service to go with the client's perception first. It is possible, for instance, that people in a certain neighborhood may think it more important to get a muddy road paved than to get a Head Start program nearby, or more useful to get a playground on the block than to have a new law on marijuana.

The DPS can help staff members maintain their commitment in the face of client apathy, ingratitude, skepticism, or lack of cooperation, or in the face of community criticism, frustration over failure or slow progress, or anxiety about using power or undermining authority.

He can help the executive director and the staff work out conflicts between the demands of a caseload and of advocacy functioning, which can become overwhelming for a worker, especially if the agency does not yet have adequate backup staff. He can help staff members sort out their individual professional priorities.

He can help staff understand that not every caseworker can be closely involved in every advocacy action, and that there are some aspects of advocacy that call for specialized expertise and knowledge not expected from every staff member. He will plan for differential use of staff in advocacy as he does in every other program offered by the agency to insure high-quality service to the clients.

Family advocacy staff

It should now be clear that a social worker at any level does not have to be designated an advocate in order to perform advocate functions. In fact, unless the agency has firmly adopted its commitment and provided the structure and the backup described above, it could be premature, even disastrous, to employ an advocate, as such. It could say to the community that the agency's concern is limited to the capacities of that one person, and if he rocks the boat too much or crosses swords with too many big givers and other important people, he will be quickly expendable.

If, however, as is fortunately much more often the case in family service, the commitment is there and the service is in fact a reality, there comes a time when the agency should employ a person who can be responsible for giving more concentrated effort to the specific areas that have been identified as urgent and for coordinating the agency's total effort to be an effective advocacy agency. The precise qualifications and job descriptions vary among family service agencies but are related appropriately to the goals of the specific program and the conditions in the community selected as the advocacy target.[17] Most agencies have employed persons with the M.S.W. degree and experience either in family service or community organization who have demonstrated leadership ability with groups and individuals. Some very effective advocates have come from allied fields —education, law, religion, rehabilitation. Most important qualifications include the ability to work with all kinds of people, an understanding of the community in which one is working, and the ability to establish credibility with the power structure as well as with the people one will serve.

Agencies that can provide strong administrative backup, including adequate consultation time and an advocacy-oriented staff, may employ an advocate with less than the master's degree level of education when a combination of personality and experience suggest the likelihood of·effective job performance. As has been noted above, the advocate is responsible to the executive director and the advocacy committee of the board, with whom he must have direct contact and to whom he must have easy access.

As an agency moves into a comprehensive external advocacy program, additional manpower will be needed. Volunteers, graduate students (in law, medicine, and theology, as well as social work), and indigenous workers who have firsthand knowledge of the oppressive conditions can assist in information-gathering and analysis of the problem. They can attend meetings, present agency positions, observe, and report to the advocacy committee. They can contribute to strategy decisions and to direct advocacy action as their individual experience, knowledge, and network of acquaintances make appropriate. All such personnel, volunteer or paid, should participate in staff development for advocacy functioning. They may have as much to teach as they have to learn.[18]

However small or large the advocacy staff, full agency support and involvement is essential to augment knowledge, supply key contacts, and provide the backing necessary to credibility.

If a necessary field of knowledge is not part of agency staff members' professional preparation, the agency can begin to repair the deficit through a staff development program, the use of consultants possessed of the missing expertise, reexamination of qualifications for employment, and advocacy with schools of social work to offer professional education that will equip social workers to operate effectively in the modern family service agency.

There is a well-established system of education and training, field placement, supervision, and agency structure to develop and back up skilled, mature, secure family caseworkers. The system is planned to promote self-understanding leading to disciplined use of self to help people. A system with this goal can be shaped to develop effective family advocates.

RISKS IN EXTERNAL ADVOCACY

Some barriers to an effective advocacy program arise from anxiety about change, fear of the unknown, need to succeed, desire to avoid criticism and controversy. Patrick V. Riley, former assistant general director of FSAA, has written:

> Advocacy can be painful for some of us and is probably threatening for most of us. Reaching out to and making common cause with people who may be unlike ourselves, extending our boundaries of concern, functioning as a community service rather than "just an agency within a community" is often not without problems, both internally and externally. To retreat after one encounter with difficulty or rejection is a temptation. It gives the opportunity to take the position, "Well, we tried. This shows what we have been saying all along, that our efforts are not wanted, not appreciated, and we should stick with what we know best." We should expect some rebuffs when we enter an area of concern in which our action role is new but in which others have been living and risking for a long time. To retreat after one, two or three rebuffs—to take our marbles and go home—would be both irresponsible and misguided. We should expect to have to earn our spurs and establish our credibility among those who have already done so.

> The Executive Director of a Family Service Agency that is and has been in the very forefront of advocacy practice faces his own anxiety directly. At a recent conference he said: "I can understand why people resist advocacy. Everything about it makes me nervous. I like my job; I want everybody to like me. Politicians scare me; reporters too. I never know what Board Members will do, even the conservatives. The conservatives are conservative on some issues and lead the charge on others. You often don't know whether your actions result in the changes produced; you just know that the changes took place. Then why do it? Because these things are in the way of families, they get in the way of trying to help families with their emotional problems; things like slum rent

gouging, school expulsions, welfare practices. The Family Service Agency is an observation post about family problems."[19]

When the agency has faced this kind of risk in the internal
advocacy process and made its commitment, it is better prepared to look at some of the outside threats and equip itself
to avoid or overcome them.

Controversy

An advocate agency can rarely retain the comfortable position of neutrality in the face of community controversy.
Obviously any time an agency comes down on one side, it
will upset, irritate, or anger those on the other side. In these
situations, the agency must weigh the risks involved in remaining silent, possibly making no enemies but also making
few friends, or of "deciding by not deciding" in the usually
futile hope that somehow the issue will go away. If it affects
families in the community, and very few controversial issues
do not, the agency can't be neutral, but must honor its commitment to serve families. The agency can decline to become deeply involved because other equally important
issues have first claim on agency resources at the time, or
because the agency is inadequately equipped to be effective
in the situation, or even because for sound reasons it is not
wise for the agency to take a leading role on a particular
issue. When such a decision is made, however, if credibility
is to be maintained, the agency must then deal openly and
honestly with those who would enlist its support and scrupulously follow through to the full extent of whatever limited commitment the agency can make.

Withdrawal of funds

An agency may be threatened with withdrawal of funds if
advocacy service takes it into areas where big givers have
interests conflicting with those of the group the agency is
serving. This possibility is an important reason for keeping
funding sources informed and, if possible, sympathetic
about agency goals. The agency board's complete support

should be enlisted through full discussion and knowledgeable decision about their willingness to stand firmly in defense of the agency's course.

CASE EXAMPLE

A caseworker, employed by a Jewish family service agency,[20] made home visits over a period of some weeks to several agency clients residing in an apartment residence for elderly people, sponsored by a local synagogue and financed by the Department of Housing and Urban Development (HUD). As her regular presence on the premises continued, she heard from many tenants other than her clients of grievances in regard to administration of the dwelling. The caseworker found that the board had general resistance to listening to grievances or making any response to individuals on the theory that elderly people always have constant and petty complaints; the tenants were assumed to have no legitimate claim on the board's attention. The rabbi who presided at the synagogue that sponsored the residence suggested that the caseworker write a letter to the board of the apartment house listing the major complaints. The rabbi also gave reluctant consent for the caseworker to attend a regular voluntary tenants' meeting for social purposes.

A notice was sent to all tenants (275 people) that the clubroom would be open to all of them for the airing of grievances for half an hour prior to the regular club meeting. Approximately 150 people attended. The caseworker identified herself and her agency. She suggested that since individual action had had no response, collective action might open lines of communication and eventually achieve results. She further suggested formation of a grievance committee. The group picked a six-member committee and approved a volunteer for the chairmanship. (There were four women and two men; three Jews and three non-Jews.) The caseworker undertook to set up a meeting of the committee with the apartment board.

Shortly thereafter tenants were informed of a rent increase. This was interpreted as an act of revenge for attempting group action. The president of the board met with the caseworker and assured her that the tenants had no legitimate complaints. In his view, they abused the services and privileges of the dwelling but there were no real problems between tenants and management, and the agency was "out of line" in getting involved. The caseworker attempted to point out mutual goals—best service for tenants. She asked for a meeting with the board but was refused. The president made it clear that he wanted the agency to stay out of the picture and to confine itself to "work in the area that Jewish Family Service was financed for," helping individuals with individual and family problems.

For two months the grievance committee met biweekly with the active support and participation of the caseworker, who established her role as an advisor ready to help them consider alternate plans of action, to go with them to present their problems, or to speak for them when they wished. The committee found a lawyer to review the rent increase. The board continued to avoid a meeting with the grievance committee but made an offer to have the chairman meet alone with the board. It was specifically stated that the agency should not be represented at any meeting with the board. These suggestions were rejected by the committee.

The struggle continued over many months. The family service board discussed the situation carefully. They considered the fact that the board members of the residence for the elderly were prominent members of the Jewish community and large supporters of the Jewish Federation, chief source of the agency's funds. There were threats of action against the agency, including the withdrawal of contributions to the federation, if it did not terminate services at the residence. The caseworker's presentation to her agency board stressed the importance for all people including the elderly to be treated with dignity and *enabled* to act responsibly in their own behalf. All people should feel that they have a way to make their problems known and to get relief from that which oppresses them. In this situation it became very evident that the agency might be the only hope for this group.

The agency board decided that the agency should continue the role of advocate. The caseworker was directed to maintain her services and to keep the agency board informed. The executive was directed to advise the federation of the problems at the residence and the agency's past involvement and continued commitment. Negotiations at executive and board levels in the federation and with the residence board were initiated. Agency board members learned firsthand something of the frustration experienced by the tenants in achieving even a hearing.

Some things did happen: The agency stood firm, the federation stood firm behind the agency, tenants' grievances were eventually addressed and most remedied; the tenants' committee became an ongoing, hale and hearty operation with a positive effect on the self-image, improved mental health, and day-to-day living conditions of many individuals in the residence. The agency was also pleased with the discovery of its own muscle and reported cheerfully that it neither fell apart under pressure nor lost funds.

Tax-exempt status

Risk to tax-exempt status is a question frequently raised. FSAA expects member agencies to abide by the law in their family advocacy programs as in all other operations. It is extremely important to know and understand the laws that govern agency activities.

Section 501(c)(3) of the Internal Revenue Code grants tax exemption to an organization "no substantial part of the activities of which is carrying on propaganda, or otherwise attempting to influence legislation, and which does not participate in, or intervene in (including the publishing or distributing of statements), any political campaign on behalf of any candidate for public office."

Legislation has been defined to include action by Congress, any state legislature, any local governing body, or the public in a referendum, initiative, constitutional amendment, or similar procedure. An organization will be regarded as attempting to influence legislation if it: (1) contacts—or urges the public to contact—the members of a legislative body for the purpose of proposing, supporting, or opposing legislation, or (2) advocates the adoption or rejection of legislation.

Legislative or propaganda activities must be substantial in order to bar an organization from tax-exempt status. Internal Revenue Service (IRS) regulations and judicial decisions fail to suggest a formula for the determination of whether an activity is substantial, but in *Seasongood* v. *Commissioner*, 227F. 2d 907 (6th Cir. 1955), it was judged that the dedication of "something less than 5 percent of the time and effort of" an organization to legislative activity "could not be deemed 'substantial' within the meaning of the section."

Legislative activities *cannot be included as an organizational purpose* but must always be seen as ancillary to the exempt purposes which must be consistent with those defined in the code: "Corporations and any community chest, fund, or foundation, organized and operated exclusively for religious, charitable, scientific, testing for public safety, library or educational purposes, or for the prevention of cruelty to children or animals . . ."

Under the present law, no agency may engage directly or indirectly in an individual's campaign for public office. This does not prohibit any individual board or staff member from campaigning on his own time or contributing his personal funds in his personal capacity as a citizen.

An individual should not use agency stationery nor the agency's address or telephone number in identifying himself while campaigning. He may identify himself as executive, staff member, or president of the board, just as a minister, rabbi, or professor is identified by his position and affiliation.

An agency may engage in legislative activity as long as its advocacy for the adoption or rejection of legislation remains an insubstantial part of its activities and the activity is directly related to the primary (and tax-exempt) purposes of the association. Such activity may include communications with a member or employee of a legislative body or with an official of the executive department of a government. It may also include efforts to affect the opinion of the general public with respect to legislation being considered by, or to be submitted imminently to, a legislative body.

Legislative activity does not include actions by executive, judicial, or administrative bodies and *there is no constraint in the Internal Revenue Code on an advocacy program in relation to any such group.* Such activity is not included in considering whether legislative activity is a substantial part of agency program.

Any attempt to "influence legislation" does not include public discussion, the general subject of which is also the subject of legislation before a legislative body, so long as such discussion does not address itself to the merits of a specific legislative proposal.

Nonpartisan analysis, study, or research and making available to the public or to governmental bodies the results of such work do not constitute carrying on propaganda or otherwise attempting to influence legislation. The analysis or study may contain recommendations, findings, or conclusions if there is a sufficiently full and fair exposition of the facts to enable the public or an individual to form an independent opinion or conclusion.

Technical advice or assistance may be given to a governmental body, or to a committee or subdivision thereof, in response to a written request by such body or subdivision. If such assistance is specifically requested on the assumption of "expert" knowledge or skill in a given area, the oral or written presentation need not qualify as nonpartisan analysis, study, or research but constitutes expert opinion.

Since legislative action is limited to the introduction, enactment, defeat, or repeal of legislation, attempting to influence legislation does not include any activity designed to bring attention to the *need* for new law nor the equitable *enforcement* of existing law nor change in the administrative interpretation of existing law through policies, rules, or regulations.

The Internal Revenue Code of 1954 and the regulations stemming from it have not changed, but the tax reform act of 1969 did create anxiety and confusion on the subject of tax-exempt status and produced a climate in which more questions are asked and more attention given to the activities of tax-exempt organizations, even though the act does not apply to family service agencies. It is also necessary to remember that political or legislative activity, in whatever amount, may bring attack from those whose interests are seen to be jeopardized in any way. If, then, the interests of agency clients are in conflict with the interests of some other group, and the agency takes a public stand in firm support of its clients, the other group may use whatever means of intimidation and retaliation come to hand. Challenging the agency's tax-exempt status could be so used, even though the agency is functioning well within the limits of IRS regulations.

The more controversial the issue and the hotter the public debate, the more likely, of course, that the opposition will look for some means of discrediting or scaring off the agency and its spokesmen. Awareness of this uncomfortable fact of life should not deter an agency from doing what it believes to be right for its constituency as long as this is permissible for tax-exempt organizations, but it does point up the importance of knowing why the issue is germane to the goals of the agency; what the facts relevant to the well-being of families and individuals are; and what the short- and long-range import of the fate of a particular piece of legislation may be for people. When the agency's board has considered these matters and has decided that the legislative issue cannot or should not be ignored, it is also essential that strategy and tactics be carefully selected with all possible expert assistance from board and staff members (as well as special consultants when needed) with administrative, legal, psychological, or political experience and know-how.

Remaining silent and inactive might well be both cowardly and unprofessional, but exercising good judgment about what to do and say is the hallmark of every profession.

Whenever possible, an agency should seek to be invited to testify rather than initiate such moves itself. Build cordial relationships with sympathetic legislators. Let them know that they can count on your help with the expert knowledge their staff needs in preparing legislation, for instance, and be generous with your appreciation of their efforts and their problems. Keep them informed of your activities and your concerns, with emphasis on the areas of their special interest. Most legislators try to become expert in something. Find out who is active in housing, public welfare, transportation, education, and family law and help these individuals see where your interests coincide and how you can be useful to one another. In turn they can often arrange for your views to be heard. A letter can be read into the record, you can be asked to appear before a committee, your reports or studies can be distributed, and so forth.

Whenever possible, act or speak jointly with other like-minded agencies rather than operating alone. You may not get as much credit if your name is one among many, even though you are doing a major share of the work, but you may well have more impact and you are less apt to be singled out for hostile attack.

Do not hesitate, when other avenues are closed, to act alone, to take initiative, to do what must be done if achievement of your goal requires it. Remember that there is a great difference between being attacked by people whose own interests are at stake and actually being investigated by the Internal Revenue Service. Even if an investigation is provoked, it must still be proved that the agency is in violation of the law before its tax-exempt status is lost.

In reports and interpretative material let it be clear that the influencing of legislation is not in itself your primary object, but that you do in fact use a variety of means to deal significantly with community problems, including the one with which the legislation is concerned. Keep records that clearly show how your resources are employed in performing all your functions, so that those employed in influencing legislation can be seen in their true perspective—as an "insubstantial" part of your total program.

The foregoing discussion of tax exemption refers to action by the agency or individuals acting and speaking *for* the agency. There is no legal limitation on any board or staff member acting or speaking as a private citizen.

In respect to safeguarding tax-exempt status under present law, an agency should not: participate, directly or indirectly, in any political campaign of a candidate for public office; or devote any substantial part of its activities to carrying on propaganda, or otherwise attempting to influence a specific piece of legislation.

It is equally important in achieving agency goals to know what the agency can legally do without jeopardizing its tax-exempt status. The agency may: engage in unlimited advocacy efforts with any individual, official, governmental body, public or voluntary organization, and the general public on any subject except specific legislative proposals during the time periods of introduction, enactment, or subsequent attempts to repeal such legislative proposals; devote an insubstantial part of its total activities to influencing legislation that is germane to its primary (and tax-exempt) purposes.

Certain advocacy efforts are not limited in any way by IRS regulations, so that an agency, to the full extent necessary to achieve its goals, may engage in the following activities: (1) seek changes in administrative practices that result from administrative interpretation of existing law through policies, rules, or regulations; (2) insist on equitable enforcement of laws; (3) advocate for the need of new law in the interest of its constituency; (4) sponsor or participate in public discussion of a general subject (such as public welfare, housing, or health care) even if it is also the subject of legislation before a legislative body, so long as such discussion does not address itself to the merits or deficiencies of a specific legislative proposal; (5) give unlimited technical consultation or assistance to a governmental body in response to its specific, written request; and (6) engage in nonpartisan analysis, study, or research and make available to the public or to governmental bodies the results of its work.

Those activities that are limited to an insubstantial amount of time (but not totally forbidden) are very specifically defined as related to legislative proposals in the process of introduction, enactment, or rejection and subsequent repeal.

Included in an agency's limited activities are: unsolicited testimony at hearings and committee meetings on specific legislative proposals; communication of opinion on specific legislative proposals to a member or employee of a legislative body or to an official of the executive department of a government; and efforts to affect the opinion of the general public with respect to specific legislative proposals.

In brief, the scope of permissible advocacy activity is far wider than the limitations, and much of the thrust of FSAA's family advocacy program is to move us all beyond the narrow view of legislative action as our only means of advocacy for the improvement of family life.

BEGINNING STEPS IN ADVOCACY

1. Get agency board involved from the beginning. Keep it fully informed and a participant in policy decisions throughout the process. The board must know the issue, the rationale for agency involvement (including the impact of the adverse conditions on families who may or may not be clients of the agency's other services), the proposed role of the agency (and how the role actually develops), the strategies selected, and the relationships of tasks assigned to various groups and individuals to the achievement of goals.

2. Know your case. Whether interviewing a family where problems are a result of a dysfunctional community, a product of personal maladjustment, or a combination of these factors, get the facts.

3. Know both sides of the case. Whether there are two opposing individuals, a family in opposition to an institution, or a neighborhood in conflict with the system, listen to both points of view and determine the strategy or treatment most likely to bring the opposing views into workable liaison.

4. Learn how the systems work. Expect the agency's knowledge base to include goals, policies, procedures, lan-

guage, and attitudes of institutions pressing on families, as well as an understanding of how family systems work.

5. Know the outside informational resources needed and use them. Seek consultation from a lawyer, state or city official, or citizen leader as planfully as from a psychiatrist or a practitioner in another social agency.

6. Find out who else is working on the problem and work toward cooperation, not confusion; collaboration and documentation, not conflict and competition. Determine who is best equipped and in the best strategic position to achieve the advocacy goal. Decide whether the agency will be more effective as leader, background supporter, or member of a coalition.

7. Check your case. Do you have all the information and documentation you need? Do you know your potential allies and your potential enemies? Are you sure of your agency's role? Is the board fully informed, appropriately involved, and thoroughly committed?

8. Make an accurate diagnosis of the problem and form an effective treatment plan or strategy for bringing about change. Mobilize allies: board members, staff, persons affected by the situation.

9. Weigh the risks to the agency and individuals and contrast these with the results to families if the agency remains inactive. Plan to protect the most vulnerable (usually the clients) from paying too high a price for too small a gain.

10. Work toward utilizing the highest level of influence and policy-making in a system necessary to remedy the problem, just as casework skills are directed to mobilizing strengths in an individual.

11. Understand that changing an institution is usually a long process involving hard work, persistence, disappointment, and only occasional moments of high drama or notable success. Compare this process with the caseworkers' expectations of movement in counseling cases.

12. Take a positive approach. Assume goodwill on the part of the system and help the system to accept that image of itself so that it must live up to it. Emphasize the ways in

which the problem is defeating the system's own goals. With the individual client, a caseworker assumes motivation to change is there and helps the client achieve insight into self-defeating behavior.

13. Work for cooperation and voluntary change but never refuse to confront if this alternative becomes necessary. Learn to work with anger, hostility, and resistance constructively as such reactions are used to help individual clients. Avoiding or denying the existence of such conditions is no more helpful to the client than taking a position in favor of sweetness, docility, or neutrality.

14. Evaluate progress. If it has been sufficient to achieve the goals, consider the factors that led to success and be generous with credit to all those who contributed, including those in the system that changed. Be sure the agency board understands what was accomplished and how it was done. If the problem is not corrected, study the situation again. What information was lacking? What were the unforeseen barriers? What mistakes in strategy were made? Do not close the case but make a new treatment plan based on experience to date.

Some suggestions for evaluation and reporting

At regular intervals an advocacy agency should report in writing the activities undertaken, the barriers encountered, the results achieved. Such reports can be made quarterly or semiannually, certainly no less than annually. They should highlight the classification of problems (housing, public welfare, health) claiming agency attention, the sources of initial agency concern (board, executive, staff member, client, outside agency or group), the kinds of intervention attempted (see "Strategies to Consider" discussed earlier), and the outcomes. If objectives have not yet been attained, some recommendation for future activity should be included. Barriers to achievement of objectives may have been encountered in the community or within the agency and should be identified, with a description of the solutions found or a recommendation for new approaches if problems still remain.[21]

In those situations that involve a coalition or at least concurrent activities by several groups toward the same end, it will not always be possible or even desirable to single out the agency's part as a primary or even a major factor in the achievement of objectives. Sometimes, for the long-range benefit of people, the system that has changed should get all the public acclaim (no matter how hard the family service agency worked to bring about change) so that it will be inspired to live up to its new reputation for real concern for those it serves.

In a coalition there is rarely equal participation. One or two members always emerge as the most active, with others serving as backup. Rarely does everybody get equal credit or, in a notably unfair world, even the credit justly deserved or appreciation for effort expended. Fortunately, the achievement of much publicity is not in itself a measure of good advocacy service. Roles do shift, differential use of methods is necessary, and the supporting group in the background of one activity may be the leader in another situation. The family agency should try to identify for itself those ways in which it contributed effectively to a successful cause in order to employ those same methods when appropriate again or suggest them to another group. Similarly, if the agency feels its contribution was ineffective, it is important to consider whether the objectives were inappropriate to the agency, the methods poorly or impulsively chosen, the implementation halfhearted or scattered. What did the agency learn that will help to avoid similar failure in the future?

Wherever possible, advocacy planning and implementation are carried through in an alliance with the persons and groups who may benefit most immediately and most directly from achieving the goals of that particular advocacy effort. As soon as possible in those situations in which the agency initiated or provided the leadership for the advocacy action, the leadership and decision-making power is transferred to these "consumer" groups. A measure of successful advocacy service in these instances is then effective transfer of leadership. An advocacy agency should give thought to ways in which it can help indigenous leadership develop and assume an effective role in achieving the further goals of the group. (See the case example above from Jewish Family Service in Trenton, New Jersey.)

Advocacy service does not yield itself to reporting by interview count nor number of clients served. The most feasible method of recording volume of work in the present state of development is probably a log of time spent in such identifiable activities as data-gathering, conference and discussion within the agency, writing of testimony or other essential documents, meetings with clients or outside groups, and so forth. A running record of contacts made (with whom and for what purpose) in reference to a cause should also be kept, with a plan for identification of leaders, decision-makers, and those who help and those who obstruct, for future reference in another situation.

Some criteria for family advocacy programs

Is the goal to change a system that is hurting people? Better service for one or a few families or more complete coverage with traditional services are not in themselves advocacy, though advocacy methods may be necessary to attain such perfectly acceptable goals.

Is the goal assurance of the right of all families to services? Pilot or demonstration projects serving a limited number of families may be an advocacy method if follow-through occurs to insure that the community in some way maintains the service and makes it universally available once the need and value have been demonstrated.

Is follow-through built in?

1. Change may not become real without monitoring to make sure that those who liked the old way are not still practicing that way even if law or policy has changed.

2. Was the change big enough to accomplish the objective?

3. Giving opportunities for people who are being hurt by a system to ventilate their feelings or sharing their concern is a service but it is not advocacy until the agency also provides avenues for changing the offending system.

4. Gathering of information is a basic step in advocacy technique but without further activity to resolve the problem thus identified and documented there has been no advocacy service.

CASE EXAMPLE

In New Hampshire in 1971, the ninety-day waiting period of parental absence for persons applying for Aid to Families with Dependent Children (AFDC) was replaced with a thirty-day period of continued absence of a parent from the home. In addition, procedures have been clarified for processing an AFDC application in instances where the thirty-day continuous absence requirement has not been met. Processing will begin immediately upon receipt of the application and an assistance check will be authorized for the earliest payroll period when all requirements are met. The applicant is responsible for certifying that the thirty-day continuous absence requirement has been met.

The manner in which this policy was changed indicates what can be achieved through the joint efforts of several agencies. Social workers and others in similar professions have in the past spent countless hours helping families deal with the problems which resulted from the ninety-day waiting period for AFDC. In the past the problems were always dealt with on a one-to-one basis, resulting in much frustration and little permanent progress. To remedy this, the social work staff at Child and Family Services of New Hampshire explained the bad effects of the ninety-day waiting period to Robert Gross (a summer law intern working jointly with New Hampshire Legal Assistance and Child and Family Services of New Hampshire). At his initiative, and through the continued efforts of New Hampshire Legal Assistance, the state Department of Health and Welfare replaced the ninety-day requirement with a thirty-day requirement.

There are two things to watch under this new procedure however:

1. The agency knows that it normally takes approximately thirty days to "process" an applicant via computer in order for the arrival of the first check, regardless of any waiting period; and

2. The recipient becomes eligible upon initial application, not after the expiration of the thirty days. Therefore, from the date of initial application to date of payment, not much more than thirty days should elapse.

It is important to keep New Hampshire Legal Assistance informed if this procedure does not operate correctly. There may be serious problems with this thirty-day rule (as opposed to no waiting period at all) and if so, further work will have to be done.

In the example cited, the agency is proud of its achievement, but aware that monitoring is necessary and that experience may indicate the need to bring about further change.

SUMMARY

Clark W. Blackburn, General Director of FSAA, in a memo to executives of accredited and provisional member agencies on December 30, 1969, said:

> I believe that the National Board and staff have made this commitment [to family advocacy] out of a deep sense of concern for all families and also out of strong conviction that FSAA has an obligation to each of you to help you carry out your commitment to your own community. Your experience will provide an important base for teaching others how to do it.
>
> As I see Advocacy, it is closely related to many of our present activities. Our knowledge base comes from our work with

thousands of individual families, our skill is in helping them to mobilize their own strengths. Both our knowledge and our skill are essential to effective advocacy. Your reports to us clearly show that a majority of you are involved in outreach programs. By themselves, they are not necessarily advocacy programs but they certainly have given you and us new insights into the causes of many family problems—the external pressure points that are destroying families. Advocacy is doing something about those causes. Outreach programs have also given you credibility and visibility in the community but the credibility will not last long if we do not take the next steps forward to change. Most of you quite correctly may say that you have always been advocates for the individual and his family. Advocacy is systematizing for every family in your community the availability of prevention or cure of the problem you saw in that one family. Advocacy is, after finding the way to help one family, establishing a system that will get that same kind of help to every family who needs it whether they get to your office or not. Even when the systems are working we still find families or individuals who because of internal problems cannot use them effectively. So we move from case to cause and back to case. Advocacy enables and extends casework; it extends the boundaries within which caseworkers see and treat pathology. Advocacy will also mitigate some of the unreal expectations and frustrations to which our profession has been subjected.

Notes

1. For other definitions developed by member agencies, see sample statements on family advocacy in Part 2, "Reports from Family Agencies."

2. Patrick V. Riley, Case to Cause—and Back to Case, 50:375, *Child Welfare* (July 1971).

3. Ibid.

4. Riley, Case to Cause, p. 376.

5. See Ellen P. Manser, *Project ENABLE: What Happened* (New York: Family Service Association of America, 1968) and Project ENABLE, *Social Casework,* 48:609–47 (December 1967).

6. *Membership Requirements* (New York: Family Service Association of America, 1964), p. 9.

7. Ibid., p. 6.

8. Family and Children's Service, Fort Wayne, Indiana, report to the board of directors, 1970.

9. For information on the operation of an agency workshop, see "Dialogue on Racism: a Prologue to Action?" in Part 3 of this manual.

10. For a fuller discussion of these ideas see "Family Advocacy—from Case to Cause," Part 3.

11. *Report of the Family Advocate Division, July, 1969, through February, 1970* (Mineola, N.Y.: Family Service Association of Nassau County).

12. For a fuller discussion of these ideas, see "Family Advocacy—from Case to Cause," Part 3.

13. Family and Children's Service, Nashville, Tennessee.

14. For a fuller discussion of these ideas see "Family Advocacy—from Case to Cause," Part 3.

15. *Report of the Family Advocate Division, July, 1969, through February, 1970* (Mineola, N.Y.: Family Service Association of Nassau County).

16. For further suggestions on board roles see "The Board of Directors as Part of the Labor Force" and "The Role of the Agency Board as Advocate for Children" in Part 3.

17. For examples of job descriptions developed by member agencies, see Part 2.

18. For specific comments on employment of nonprofessionals, see "Calling It Advocacy Does Not Make It So," Part 3.

19. Riley, Case to Cause, pp. 380, 381.

20. Jewish Family Service, Trenton, New Jersey.

21. For examples of regular reports from advocacy agencies, see Part 2.

Part Two

Reports from Family Agencies

STATEMENTS ON
FAMILY ADVOCACY

Child and Family Services of Connecticut, Inc.
Hartford, Connecticut

Child and Family Services of Connecticut believes that family
advocacy as a service program is a means by which our total
agency can relate to others. This kind of centralized service
draws upon board, staff, and volunteers as well as involving
other organizations and groups in enhancing the effectiveness
of each in serving all citizens of the communities with which
we are identified.

Social workers and mental health professionals have for
some years felt the need of a family advocacy program.
Family advocacy is a nationwide concern. Family Service
Association of America, of which Child and Family Services
is a member agency, has encouraged the establishment of
family advocacy programs among its member agencies. The
recommendations of the Joint Commission on Mental Health
of Children included proposals for a child advocacy system.

In order to learn more about advocacy, Child and Family
Services included in its 1970–1971 training program a workshop on family advocacy led by S. Frances Brisbane, ACSW,
a staff member of FSAA; Robert Sunley, ACSW, Family
Service Association of Nassau County, New York; and Michael

Porter, South Green Neighborhood Center, Hartford. Board, staff, and volunteers of the family agencies of Hartford participated in this workshop. A workshop on family advocacy was also held at the time of the last annual meeting, and family advocacy was included as a priority on the agenda of the agency's family service committee.

Child and Family Services of Connecticut offers many services to clients in several communities in the state. Within these service programs caseworkers have always interacted with a network of other service-providing agencies to meet the needs of specific clients. A program of family advocacy is another important service which this agency can offer to the communities it serves. It is based on our acknowledgement that Child and Family Services is itself a social institution whose aim has been to provide a better social environment. It is motivated by the responsibility we feel to interact clearly and effectively with other agencies to improve the opportunities and resources for human development in our communities.

The caseworkers and mental health professionals of our agency have struggled time after time to rectify the wrongs suffered by our clients. Sometimes a caseworker succeeds, often through some personal contact with a counterpart in the offending social institution, but he is only too aware of and further frustrated by the fact that ten or one hundred other people continue to suffer for lack of such influential intervention. The caseworker's action on behalf of one client does not bring about any basic change in how clients are served. It is the gap between rectifying injustices on a case-by-case method and the failure to alter basic institutional methods which demonstrates the need for a program of family advocacy.

WHAT IS FAMILY ADVOCACY?

Family advocacy can best be defined in terms of its basic goal, which is healthy individuals plus families living in a society where attitudes and environmental conditions are supportive, not hostile to human growth; where opportunities and resources for maximum human development are available and accessible to every individual and family. In essence, the program should attempt to effect a change in institutions and systems so that they work on behalf of individuals and families, not against them. The family advocacy program would move the agency's avowed concern from "case to cause."

In committing the agency as a whole to an advocacy program, the client changes. He is not only that individual or that family who is in direct contact with us but also all the potential families who suffer from the same institutional problem. A commitment to action on the behalf of families is not new to Child and Family Services. The methods of advocacy are not in themselves wholly new. Many ask: "Is advocacy a new name for doing an old thing?" In the case of Child and Family Services, it seems to combine new and old methods and policies. It would be a new name to call the action this agency took in supporting the legalized abortion bill. It would be a new name to call the actions which resulted in hospital clinic patients receiving appointments rather than all reporting first thing in the morning to wait endlessly for medical attention. It would be a new name to call our agency stand on making birth control information available to clients. It would be a new thing to do if this agency, which has often interceded to get one family better housing, took a public stand on housing conditions and the enforcement of housing codes, when feasible. It would be a new thing to do if this agency, which has so often prevailed upon schools not to expel one confused child, took a public stand on the disciplinary method of school exclusion.

In summary, family advocacy is directed at altering institutional policies and practices so that they will be supportive of individuals and families.

METHODS OF FAMILY ADVOCACY

Issues, in advocacy, are created to focus attention, to foster concern, to initiate action, to promote justice; and family advocacy means to do whatever one must do in the interest of the agency's constituency. In light of this, of concern to staff and board members are the actual techniques employed in advocacy programs, the methodology of such a program. Some people have a vague notion that advocacy means sit-ins, protests, picketing. Others envision endless petitions. Many are concerned with the effects such activities have upon the regard the community has for our agency.

The methodology for advocacy includes: studies and surveys, expert testimony, case conferences with other agencies, interagency committees, educational methods, position-taking, administrative redress, demonstration projects, direct contacts with legislators and officials, coalition groups focused on specific objectives and assisted by agencies, client groups, petitions, and persistent demands short of harassment. The procedure is to go through existing channels for redress, to cooperate, and to assist the social institution to function in a way which is healthy for families. Demonstrations and protests are methods in the repertoire of advocacy. However, these are measures which would be used only as a last resort.

As in any effective service program, the methodology employed for any issue is carefully selected for that change plan. For example, an effort to challenge a state law usually will require a massive effort, on many levels and with various methods, whereas challenging a practice of a local organization may be accomplished through such means as meetings, pressures, client groups, and administrative redress. The position from which we act should be with compassion for those whose needs are being neglected, not from a position of righteous criticism of social institutions, or of concern with the effects that our involvement may have upon our receiving funds from any particular source.

EXAMPLES OF SUCCESSFUL ADVOCACY

Catholic Family Services of Hartford worked toward keeping a free-lunch program in an urban school for black and Spanish-speaking children. It was felt that in order to cut down on the school dropout rate, it was imperative to make provision for lunches. With board approval, the agency's advocacy committee organized a widely representative committee from the black and Puerto Rican neighborhoods, board and staff members of other agencies, and public health doctors. This committee met with the superintendent of the local school board and the state education department's school program consultants. It was learned there were funds available for school lunches if the local board of education applied for them. The local board of education did not have the funds for equipment and personnel to carry out the program. The family service agency, with its broad community-supported committee, collected funds from a number of individuals and agencies to start the program. Within a few months the lunch program became part of the total school program.

In another community, agencies became aware of the long hours clinic patients spent waiting to be seen at the hospital clinics. Our agency, as well as other agencies in the community, met with the administrators of all the hospitals in the city to try to change this situation. The clinic personnel were vitally interested since trying to serve so many people at once made their work very difficult. An appointment schedule was worked out so that all clinic patients were given individual appointments, and waiting lines at the clinics were eliminated.

Social workers are in daily contact with the poor and recognize when their needs are not being met. Public assistance benefits are low. The population of federally aided welfare programs has never included all the needy. The working poor and the employable but unemployed poor are usually excluded from potential eligibility because of the variety of federal, state, and local eligibility requirements.

Much is happening that is of concern to all private agencies in our own state in regard to public welfare. Members from many community agencies have formed a coalition committee to discuss with the commissioner of welfare the implications for welfare recipients of recent policy changes. Two vital issues concern rent restrictions and flat grant monthly allowances.

In adopting an advocacy program we must be aware that there will be differences of opinion as to how to tackle many of our community problems. There will be criticism and possible retaliation at times, as our advocacy program begins to function. However, we feel our agency committee, as is suggested in this policy statement, is organized in such a way as to be able to cope with any criticism.

STRUCTURE

The commitment of the agency to action on behalf of families is obviously the cornerstone of an advocacy program. But a workable structure for advocacy needs to be established. The structure must be one which can and does involve the entire agency, including staff, board, and volunteers, in an ongoing activity. The committee feels the first step is the appointment of a board committee composed of members from board and staff and volunteers from the community. This committee would be responsible for determining the areas of advocacy in which the agency is to become involved. Once such a committee is established within the agency, the next step would be to consider the forming of an interagency council. Such a council would tie the four family agencies together, as well as provide each agency with the opportunity to act as a separate body if it so desires. Although the model suggested relates specifically to Hartford, the committee feels it is applicable to any of the communities in which the agency is involved. Schematically, the structure would be as follows:

Interagency Advocacy Council

Full-time advocate

Child and Family Services of Connecticut	Catholic Family Service	Jewish Family Service	Family Service Society
staff assistant board representative	staff assistant board representative	staff assistant board representative	staff assistant board representative

There are advantages to this approach both for the specific agency and for the four agencies together acting as the interagency advocacy council. The advantages for our agency are as follows:

1. We would be able to implement a program for family advocacy while negotiations for the development of an interagency advocacy council are proceeding.

2. We would have the capabilities to carry out an advocacy program concerning those issues which are of concern only to our agency.

3. It would provide a liaison with existing advocacy programs in other agencies when our interests coincide.

The role of the staff person would be to provide information for the board advocacy committee for policy-making, to help implement board decisions, and to develop and execute educational seminars for our own staff. When the interagency advocacy council becomes a reality, the staff person would serve as our liaison with the council.

In relation to the council, the advantages of this approach are as follows: (1) avoids overlapping and duplication of efforts among the four family agencies; (2) reduces cost for each agency, as the cost for the full-time advocate would be shared by the four agencies; and (3) increases the likelihood that efforts at retaliation would be lessened since four agencies, not one, would be involved.

Family Service of Greater New Haven, Inc.
New Haven, Connecticut

The basic goal of the advocacy program of Family Service of Greater New Haven, a community counseling and psychiatric service agency, is healthy individuals and families living in a society where attitudes and environmental conditions are supportive of, not hostile to, human growth; where opportunities and resources for maximum human development are available and accessible to every individual and family. In essence, the program attempts to effect a change in institutions and systems so that they work on behalf of individuals and families—not against them.

The fact is that social workers helping people in trouble have long been aware that institutional defects in our society tend to obstruct if not destroy families. Therefore, the advocacy program of the agency, in alliance with other interested groups, hopes to be able to systematize for every family in the community the prevention or cure of negative factors which destroy individuals or families. The program is not limited to the poor, to those of limited income, or to minority groups, though, because they suffer most intensely, they will receive priority.

The advocacy program at Family Service of Greater New Haven functions through a five-member committee comprised of staff and administration, which collects and evaluates pertinent information from individual and family experiences that point to areas where institutional changes may be necessary. The committee works closely with various committees of the board, other agencies, and community groups.

Committee members belong to such community agencies as the Urban League, Human Relations Council, Black Coalition, Citizens Commission to Develop Quality Education, Community Council, and Central Labor Council—so we are aware of the trend in the community and can work with other organizations.

We see ourselves working along with groups and individuals who desire our service in a variety of ways. Because of our training and know-how we can often facilitate action. We have objectivity which can help sort out vital issues of the situation and help focus the problem. Sometimes we can define clearly whether a problem is based on a specific situation or whether there are more serious implications which should be acted upon. Often we have the resources to make available copies of laws and regulations, so that it becomes possible to move ahead quickly. Existing agencies are accessible to us and because of this we can facilitate action with a minimum of delay. We have provided our meeting room and secretarial service to the groups with whom we work.

In short many of our casework skills are used in advocacy:

A problem is presented; it is examined and evaluated, using the professional resources which we have; solutions are suggested; and, lastly, a plan is chosen by the group which presents the problem. We are then available to give whatever assistance we can to produce such changes in our society as can bring about optimum family life.

The advocacy committee has focused on the following areas:

1. The agency itself has taken a look at where it is and where it could become more responsive to the current scene.

2. During the recent teachers' strike, community groups shared with us the need for day care for children who could not attend school and whose mothers were at work. The advocacy committee spearheaded planning for day care facilities for elementary school youngsters.

3. The committee addressed itself to the concept of fair rent guidelines for families with children, those on limited income, and those who live in substandard quarters.

4. Intervention with state and city welfare officials on behalf of clients took place in various ways. When it was learned that state and federal guidelines were not always applied to Connecticut residents, we worked with this information with the New Haven and Milford Welfare Moms who attended a Health, Education and Welfare (HEW) hearing in Boston. Consumer advocacy on the part of several welfare recipients has also taken place. Results in many of these areas were encouraging.

5. The committee has collected some data on how individuals and families are affected by our jails. We have talked with inmates at the jail and met with a legal assistance counsel to bring case material into light. The inmates of the jail asked us to get together families and ex-inmates and we are participating with other community agencies in this. Our ultimate goal is to contribute greater awareness of the human needs of the prison inmates and work with their families.

6. Particularly in legislative years we have supported legis-

lation in many areas, especially in day care. We are aware of the limits of existing day care programs and support increased facilities along these lines.

7. A member of the committee attended a two-and-a-half-day conference on polarization in New Haven. Since that meeting the agency has played an active role with the Commission on Equal Opportunity to have the mayor acknowledge and act upon a report on minority employment.

8. The committee has participated in workshops on advocacy in connection with social agencies and the University of Connecticut School of Social Work. We have lent support to the school lunch program and the Residential Youth Center.

Child and Family Services of New Hampshire
Manchester, New Hampshire

> Through family advocacy we are trying to eliminate root causes of problems which are destructive to family life. In the past, we have interceded to help individuals obtain fair treatment from public institutions, many of which were unresponsive. This repeated individual intervention by the staff of Child and Family Services was often ineffective in securing relief for the countless other persons faced with essentially similar problems. Through our family advocacy program we are identifying and attempting to resolve classes of problems which confront families and individuals.

With this new approach we do not ignore the fact that people often have individual problems which can cause family crises. But as advocates, we are going to do more for people than just help them cope with the existing systems and institutions. Institutions and systems which were originally designed to serve people have too often become causes of problems for the very people they were designed to help. Or, in many instances, existing problems have been aggravated. As advocates, we are going to work with and for families and children to make the existing systems and institutions work for these individuals. Recognition of the need to help people change institutions, rather than to help people cope with institutions, means recognition of the need for modifying or adding to the ways we ourselves have helped people solve their problems in the past.

While our agency works constantly to be alert to all situations, systems, and institutions which through malfunctioning help to cause problems for families and children, our family advocacy program has concentrated its efforts in four general areas. In order to more adequately meet the needs of families and children, we have been working to establish a more equitable system for administration and distribution of local public assistance; we have been working to ease the housing shortage in New Hampshire; we have been trying to facilitate the process by which foster children are either returned to their homes or made available for adoption; and we have attempted to insure that pregnant students be allowed to remain in school until they graduate.

New Hampshire is suffering from a severe housing shortage. Staff members at Child and Family Services spend considerable time counseling individuals and families whose emotional problems are made more severe by lack of adequate housing. The absence of any tenants' rights group helps to accentuate a situation which we believe leads to a great deal of destruction of family life. We are working to establish tenants' rights in New Hampshire.

General financial assistance in the state is funded and regulated on a local basis. There are over 200 separate programs of local public welfare assistance. For the overwhelming majority of these programs there are no written standards of eligibility, and there are no written standards of assistance. Thus, applicants for financial assistance at the local level are arbitrarily given or denied assistance. We are working to see that local public welfare departments establish some written eligibility requirements and written standards of assistance.

Family Service of the Cincinnati Area
Cincinnati, Ohio

SOME SUGGESTED GUIDELINES
A family advocacy program:
1. Should have a clear family aspect, focus, goal;
2. Should be within the agency's area of competence;
3. Should be solid and factually based on the agency's own services and verified evidence;
4. Should be rooted in rights, as well as needs of a family or families;
5. May focus on the rights of a single family, or a group of families, or a whole class of families;
6. Should focus on removing the obstacle for all families, rather than for a particular client family; and
7. Should begin with assessment of the family's (or group of families') capacity and potential for using help or readiness for success in effecting removal of its obstacle.

If the prognosis for success is poor according to the preceding list, ways should be weighed in which the agency can actively assist by promoting or participating in group family advocacy, by caseworker, administration, or board.

If a client family cannot advocate effectively, ways should be weighed in which the agency as an institution, preferably in conjunction with others, or if necessary, alone, can advocate for the necessary system change.

The program should be carefully studied for its appropriateness to the agency, probability of success, potential allies, and strategy, *before* embarking. Only those causes for which the agency envisions the client family or the large group or the agency as able to bear the risks, with a likelihood of success, should be launched; family advocacy demands careful strategic assessment and—because an action may last over a long period—timely reevaluations.

Differential family advocacy roles for caseworkers, administration, and board should be defined. Each should review its present duties and methods in the light of these tenets. It is likely that these refinements will require prolonged attention and the acquisition of additional skills.

The spirit in which we approach family advocacy will determine whether we use it to combine our best talents and our dedication to the family (1) in practical activities to aid more client families to break out of constricting circumstances; (2) to support and join them in the process of relieving the lives of families in general from these restrictions; and (3) to add to community understanding of how our whole system of services and opportunities may actually block family health for many, and how this system can be improved.

An agency's credentials for the second and especially the third of these achievements will derive largely from its staff's success with the first, which calls for hard work to sharpen direct services to clients.

The road ahead is very long. We can expect failures and successes, and may learn much from both. How each chooses to run the course will make mere rhetoric of *family advocacy*, or will give it meaning.

Family and Children's Service
Nashville, Tennessee

The long-range goals, published in December 1969, emphasize the future role of the agency as an advocate in stating, "Family and Children's Service is dedicated to preserving the dignity of the individual and the strength of the family. So it is impelled to keep closer company with individuals and groups in our society who are fighting the causes of social ills. It is called upon to ally itself with an enlarged corps of professions and disciplines who are laboring to rescue persons and families from poverty, degradation, and injustice. Our agency must become, then, an informed and competent spokesman on social issues; for it must challenge the community to create conditions which enhance wholesome family life. It must place the problems of family welfare upon the community's conscience. In its advocacy of constructive measures on behalf of families, Family and Children's Service must earn the right to be consulted about proposed changes in social welfare programs."

Advocacy should be a valid function of the agency equal in importance to the services we now provide. Family and Children's Service must extend its focus to include community conditions and practices that are harmful to or interfere with individual and family life. There are conditions and institutional practices in our community that contribute to individual and family dysfunctioning that will require new methods and techniques in addition to the traditional casework approach.

The incorporation of a family advocacy program by Family and Children's Service will involve a reordering of services and structure: (1) a reordering of priorities to make it possible for staff to give time to problems of advocacy; (2) the extension of communication with other agencies and community groups to facilitate cooperative action, and (3) the designation of a staff member to fill the position of staff advocacy specialist.

STRUCTURE AND PROCESS

Staff advocacy specialist
The advocacy specialist is a staff person who is selected to take leadership and responsibility for carrying out the agency's advocacy program. This will entail a reduced caseload in order for him to devote the bulk of his time to advocacy. He will be chairman of the staff advocacy committee and serve as liaison between staff, board, and community organizations.

Staff advocacy committee
The staff advocacy committee, composed of a minimum of three staff members who will also serve as staff representatives to the public issues committee, will gather pertinent information from the staff, and screen and select issues to recommend to the public issues committee. Some problems can be dealt with simply by staff intervention. A staff member may also take leadership in a project of interest, using the staff advocacy specialist as a consultant and as a person

to account to. It will be each staff member's responsibility to identify and refer advocacy problems to this committee.

Public issues committee

The public issues committee is made up of board and staff advocacy committee members, including the staff advocacy specialist. The public issues committee will review issues recommended by the staff advocacy committee, or any board member or board committee, and select those appropriate for agency action. It will develop a plan of action and will assign responsibilities. The chairman of the public issues committee will bring the committee's recommendations to the board for discussion and approval of suggested action. In case of emergencies, anticipated action must be cleared by the executive director with the executive committee.

Each position relating to advocacy, so approved by the board, will be put in writing for board and staff in order that Family and Children's Service will have a clear record of its current advocacy program.

JOB DESCRIPTIONS

Family Service Association of Nassau County
Mineola, New York

Different patterns for staff advocacy are possible, depending on agency size, funding, staff interests, and other considerations, of which the following are examples:

1. A full-time staff position of family advocate, or a department of advocacy headed by the family advocate. This position, as recently established at Family Service Association of Nassau County through a foundation grant, is initially projected to include two main functions: first, to work with staff, providing consultation on action on behalf of indi-

vidual clients, or handling certain situations directly, and compiling case material on problems for the public issues committee. In addition, the family advocate will work to involve the staff in further action, such as the formation of client groups in regard to problems, participation on committees and in hearings, and other forms of action. It should be noted that clerical staff in social agencies have or develop a commitment to the purposes of social work and should have the opportunity to ally themselves as agency people as well as in private life.

As a second major focus, the family advocate acts as the staff consultant to the public issues committee. He helps them define priority problems through case material and background information and through bringing in officials and others who are involved in the problems; he works with them to set guidelines and steps for action, to think through implications, to review what has been done, and to evaluate methods. The family advocate may act as agency spokesman and as liaison to officials or legislators. He may act as agency representative with coalition groups and community groups, as consultant to client groups, or as advisor to staff or board people who carry out these functions.

2. Variation on the establishment of a full-time family advocate might be a part-time position instead. Or an indigenous worker might fill the position, which in turn might require the investment of more staff and consultation time but bring other advantages, such as better contact with local poverty groups.

3. A current staff member might be assigned in agencies where the budget does not permit expansion of staff at present. Or a part-time assignment could be made, as an expedient only, since the conflict between demands of a caseload and of the advocacy function would be frequent and onerous for the worker.

4. A staff committee might be formed, with a chairman bearing responsibility for the advocacy function, but delegating items of work to committee members. This method has the advantage of involving more staff directly, keeping

the advocacy function related to the casework, and keeping the staff in direct contact with the board committee, but it could present difficulties in carrying-out actions, as well as in the demands upon the worker's attention and time mentioned above.

It may be possible with the above patterns for the agency to obtain graduate social work students to lend much-needed manpower. Students can, for example, do much of the background work which is time-consuming for the caseworker but essential to the advocacy function. Some schools of social work, in preparing generic workers, may find this a highly desirable type of placement, since it can provide the student with selected cases related to advocacy, with client groups to work with in connection with the advocacy, and with the community organization and action experience.

In agencies where a separate position of family advocate cannot be established, staff members carrying the functions in one of the patterns suggested should have access directly to the responsible board committee and work with that committee. Otherwise the resulting delays in cross-communication and lack of clarity may result in hamstringing any action.

One or more specialists may be needed to act as consultants to the advocacy program; this may include consultation on agency structuring and functioning for advocacy, orientation to clientele, assisting client groups, and defining areas of action and strategies.

Family Service/Travelers Aid
Norfolk, Virginia

TITLE: FAMILY ADVOCATE-COMMUNITY ORGANIZER
The task of the family advocate-community organizer is to strengthen the lives of groups of individuals or families who are hampered by the malfunctioning of a societal system which could be enhancing their ability to be more

productive members of society; through consultation, to encourage and assist other staff members in focusing their knowledge, skills, and service toward remedying the community systems that are hampering their assigned families from leading a more satisfying life; to develop self-help groups from families receiving agency direct service that they may benefit from leadership in community organization methods; and to assist agency committees to focus upon community problems that impede satisfactory family life.

Duties and responsibilities

1. Consultation with staff: initiate discussions with agency direct-service personnel to determine the nature and extent of the various external community activities that actually or potentially threaten the adequate functioning of the family or individual; analyze and group these various external community resources known to the total agency to be dysfunctioning according to community systems (e.g., health, education, welfare, employment, day care); gather information (legislative statutes, regulations, policies, interpretations, licensing practices) about these dysfunctioning systems; and make recommendations or assist the direct-service personnel on courses of action to correct the dysfunctioning systems.

2. Direct service to family groups: carry the community organization responsibility of developing an advocacy group from the families selected from the entire agency direct-service staff; carry the responsibility of reaching out to families in a neighborhood to assist them in organizing and functioning as an advocacy group; and where these family groups select community systems that may be malfunctioning, the family advocate shall actively involve the board of directors, administration, and direct-service staff in the group assignments.

3. Direct service to agency groups: bring to the attention of the agency those conditions in the community that are having a deleterious effect upon family life and in which

no direct-service staff member(s) have responsibility for an advocacy group and carry the responsibility for planning, developing, and directing an agency group consisting of affected individuals and families, board members, and interested citizens, toward the resolution of a community systems problem.

4. On public issues: analyze, interpret, and coordinate agency activities that pertain to local, state, and federal legislation that will strengthen family life.

Qualifications

1. Master's degree in social work, plus satisfactory completion of Social Worker II classification within the agency, which includes demonstrated community organization competence in self-responsible practice of high quality. This is acquired through supervised experience which generally takes five years.

2. A job candidate having a master's degree in social work may have had employment in other social agencies. There should have been regular and closely supervised experience which demonstrated use of community organization concepts and competence in self-responsible practice of high quality. This is acquired through supervised experience which generally takes five years.

3. It is recognized that other professions that deal extensively in human relations may produce suitable educational and employment experiences and personal qualities that may lend themselves to this position classification. A job candidate must have graduated from an accredited college or university with a master's degree in education, psychology, sociology, or a bachelor's degree in divinity. The content of the courses studied in human relations will be the major influence in deciding upon the educational qualification. A job candidate must have had not less than ten years of demonstrated employment experience in his chosen profession using the educational criteria. There must have been demonstrated employment experience in use of community organization concepts. A mature per-

sonality that can offer leadership with groups and individuals must be demonstrated from the work experience.

United Charities of Chicago
Chicago, Illinois

**TITLE: ASSOCIATE EXECUTIVE DIRECTOR FOR
SOCIAL ADVOCACY**

The task of the associate executive director for social advocacy is to develop, plan for, and administer a program designed to insure that community institutions or systems support the coping capacities and the development of families and individuals, rather than impinge upon them. He is responsible to the executive director.

Responsibilities

1. Works with staff and board to plan and develop an effective social advocacy program for the agency.

2. Gives leadership to the social advocacy committee of the board in developing policies and plans to effect change; interprets social advocacy situations to the committee.

3. Compiles, analyzes, and evaluates situations where a direct connection exists between the experience, special knowledge, and skills of the agency and the issue at hand.

4. Gives leadership to staff to define situations where agency clients are suffering injustices due to inadequacies or limitations of social institutions.

5. Plans with the director of the family service, legal aid, and camping programs to insure that the social advocacy program is carried out collaboratively with those services and in the context of overall agency objectives to strengthen and develop families and individuals.

6. Participates in agency-wide planning for program development.

7. Acts as a consultant, or obtains additional resources, to assist staff in effectively implementing their advocacy function.

8. Establishes effective working relationships with a wide range of community institutions and organizations, including both public and private social agencies.

9. Initiates and makes recommendations on the departmental budget to the executive director and the public affairs committee.

10. Supervises staff assigned to the department.

11. Works with all administrative departments, such as public relations and statistics, in carrying out the responsibilities of the department.

12. May plan special projects and work with fund-raising consultants to secure funding.

Qualifications
An advanced degree in the political or social sciences or equivalent experience and a minimum of eight years in a social agency, with experience in work with the community.

Part Three

Selected Readings

Contributors

S. Frances Brisbane is southwestern regional representative, Family Service Association of America, Dallas, Texas.

David R. Hunter is executive director, Stern Family Fund, New York, New York.

Howard Hush is executive director, Family Service of Metropolitan Detroit, Detroit, Michigan.

Joseph H. Kahle is executive director, Family Counseling Service, Seattle, Washington.

Michael J. Kami is president, Corporate Planning Associates, Lighthouse Point, Florida.

Charles S. Levy, D.S.W., is professor, Wurzweiler School of Social Work, Yeshiva University, New York, New York.

Pauline D. Lide, D.S.W., is professor, School of Social Work, University of Georgia, Athens, Georgia.

Mrs. Irwin C. Lieb is board member, Child and Family Service, Austin, Texas.

Mary J. McCormick, Ph.D., is professor and director, Social Welfare Program, University of San Francisco, San Francisco, California.

Joseph McDonald is executive director, Family Service of the Cincinnati Area, Cincinnati, Ohio.

Robert Sunley is associate director, Family Service Association of Nassau County, Mineola, New York.

Edwin F. Watson is executive director, Family Service Association of Metropolitan Toronto, Toronto, Ontario.

THE BOARD OF DIRECTORS AS PART OF THE LABOR FORCE

S. Frances Brisbane

In the establishment of an advocacy program, "business as usual" is counterproductive. Priorities for the use of board members' time, in addition to that of the professional staff members, must be established. The time that board members spend on major fund-raising affairs and on compiling long lists of friends and patrons could often be spent getting pledges for involvement. Such pledges could be secured from neighbors and friends to work with board members on committees to examine school textbooks, to establish a low-cost community dental clinic, or to sponsor free legal advisory services. On each committee, a board member could share the chairmanship with a nonboard member. This approach would involve people for their talents rather than their money. It would spread community responsibility around in the community.

People with a great deal of knowledge and competence in particular areas, but with little time to serve on boards and even less money to contribute for constantly evolving worthwhile causes, could offer services that would be practically impossible to purchase. After a period of operation, funds could be sought from major funding sources to expand advocacy projects which would evolve into service-giving programs and open up jobs on many levels, employing residents indigenous to the community.

Each committee might have its own stationery with names and other agency connections or area of expertise listed for identification purposes. Several committees could bring the agency greater publicity and more accountability, while producing sources of knowledge, information, prestige, and potential board leadership. These friends of the community (as opposed to friends of the agency) may be greater assets to the agency than any amount of money, glitter, and publicity achieved by traditional methods.

It is conceivable that a small agency with twenty board members and limited staff could give birth to important autonomous committees working on specialized problems or in specialized areas. The agency would continue to benefit from the groups' efforts and would have built many human resources. We followed this general idea at FSAA, and we now count Plays for Living, IMPAC (Information, Management, Processing, Analysis, and Communication for voluntary social agencies) and National Study Service among our most precious assets.

Variations of the above format could include community people from low socioeconomic backgrounds. The committees could derive a wealth of experiences from people who are subjected or potentially subjected to the problem area chosen for attention.

The board-staff advocacy committee to whom the citizen-board committee is responsible should retain administrative control of the way information and results are used. Inherent in this arrangement is that the administration of activities which feed directly into the lives of clients, as well as others, should be professionally and administratively supervised, like all other functions within the agency's operation. Staff assigned to an advocacy committee could coordinate the group's activities and serve as liaison. This would ensure that the results and status of action of the citizen-board committee are readily available for daily use in the staff's work with individuals and families.

While the citizen-board committee may meet without staff participation—though with staff available for consultation in the community and at times convenient for the group—the advocacy committee as a total agency operation should meet at the agency. Advocacy committee reports should be made at board meetings and staff meetings. The input and cooperative efforts of the staff and board would flow back to the advocacy committee for incorporation.

In the early stages of the advocacy committee's operation, it may be useful to have several board meetings devoted to the discussion of advocacy with the advocacy committee presenting information, seeking advice, learning of particular board members' interest in specific areas, and in general keeping the total board involved in the initial period when it is likely that there could be much misunderstanding and need for interpretation and clarification. The same approach for the same purposes should be duplicated at staff meetings.

The spirit of advocacy is to have members participate on committees to learn the vital statistics of the local community, county, and state. This function could be the responsibility of a public issues committee, which too frequently takes on global issues, lodged in national or international areas of concern, and discharges its commitment by writing a letter to the president or a senator, with no attempt to seek results or follow through. While such activity is worthwhile and should continue, it is not enough for a local agency to extend its reach beyond the boundaries of the community, and perhaps its immediate responsibility, when it speaks out to seek new laws and revision of old laws. Our target of change should primarily be in the local community, county, or state that holds the answer to many of the problems of "people hurting the most in our society." The family service agency is in a position to exert more influence over local issues and local legislators—just by the agency's reputation and location. In this regard, change could come about not because of active lobbying but by subtly conveying a message that board members, exercising their civic options, will use their votes to express their feelings about the community in which they live.

The vital statistics which a committee or several subcommittees of the public issues committee could seek are many and these should be used to establish advocacy services on a priority basis, in keeping with the community demand for institutional change, not on an agency-interest basis. The public—and not so public—records of all the major institutions should be viewed. For example, statistics on education may reveal staggering information: A high proportion of children who graduate from ghetto high schools are not qualified to go on to college; school dropouts among minorities are heavily weighted with males rather than females; fifty black male children to every one nonblack child, male or female, at the fourth-grade level, are referred to family agencies and child guidance clinics for a variety of reasons; special classes for slow learners are filled with two-thirds of all black and Spanish-surnamed children in attendance in a school where the minority group is less than 2 percent of the total school population; not one Indian child over a ten-year period graduated from the white, suburban school system to which he was bused; all black children entering suburban schools over a ten-year period, without any tests, were placed in the fourth track where they remained until they became dropout statistics, vocational education enrollees, or obtained a general diploma attesting to their school attendance rather than academic attainment. (These statistics have been *manufactured* to highlight a point, and the value of research and the acquisition of facts and statistics is directly related to the interpretation of them.)

With such information as this, it would not be difficult to convince the correction and rehabilitation institutions that unless they make more demands on boards of education while the latter have these children in charge, in a few years the cost to the taxpayer will be tripled. Nor should it be difficult to suggest to the community that its fears of crime committed by the discontented, misplaced minority adult will force privileged whites into private schools only to return home through crime-ridden communities or to areas from which they feel as compelled to move every three to five years as must the ghetto resident who is dislocated from urban renewal sites. In short, the education system of the community becomes nonfunctional for *all* children.

The family service agency may find itself party to the education problem by accepting all children referred by the schools, without helping the schools examine their system of educating minorities. Helping the minority child adjust to a predictable school status that prepares minority children for institutional dependency is no easier than helping the system to change. A meaningful discussion with school officials with a view toward readjusting their systems to accommodate the needs and differences of minority children for the good of the child and the community could produce better schools for every child. In some agencies, the statistics taken from its own case load may be sufficient to raise questions concerning referral trends of minority youngsters, warranting a frank discussion about the possibility of the problem being twofold: school and child, or the problem child being the victim of racist institutional practices.

Another board committee could review coroner's reports for the causes of death, and age at death, of citizens who lived in the town's most blighted area or were part of transient labor force. These communities could be characterized as having inadequate housing without proper refrigeration facilities in the summer, heat in the winter, and accessible health services. The information on the ages and causes of death compared to the death docket of the privileged could occasion concern, commitment, and action on housing legislation, establishment of health codes, building satellite health clinics, or regulation of labor laws.

A board committee, especially in a rich suburban community where the poor are in the minority and may live in a pocket of poverty, may find that their fellow citizens suffer much more than their urban counterparts. Why? There are usually fewer public facilities to accommodate their needs. In many such communities, lack of public transportation is the key to many other difficulties which the poor must encounter daily. The hospital, shopping centers, industrial sites, railroad representative, college administration, social service agencies, library, and other institutions could be asked to cooperate in a study to determine the feasibility of providing public transportation to the above places, with bus routes originating in or passing through the poverty area. It would be a public service to the total community and poor people in particular. The exorbitant taxi fares which the poor pay—usually for taxis that are far short of the demand—could be used on more basic and enriching items and activities. The bus company would realize a profit and the mobility of the poor could be matched to their desire and need.

How does an agency count the numbers of people served through its advocacy effort? It may not be as easy as counting the direct-service case loads, but this is no reason to believe an accurate count is not possible. Nor is an estimated account without accountability. For example, in New York State a law legalizing abortions was passed. A family service agency in a New York town which had worked hard and long on getting this law passed—motivated by its concern about the high incidences of death from illegal abortions or the number of cases of parents and their unwanted children seen in therapy—could have researched the number of deaths over a five-year period prior to the enactment of the law. If they had found that deaths attributed to abortions had risen steadily, and that after abortions became legal the figure dropped to a very few or none, it is more than conceivable that the agency could credit itself with having saved from death at least the average number of people who died in previous years. This figure would bear a close relationship to the number of clients seen and unseen in other local communities who benefitted from advocacy in the area of legalizing abortions. The agency could justifiably link its efforts with all other individuals, groups, and agencies in other New York areas as the responsible forces in coalition to reduce deaths and anguish on a statewide basis.

The field of medicine, from which social work patterned much of its work, constantly makes available information about the diminishing number of people afflicted by a disease because the medical researchers have found a miracle drug. No one is encouraged to speculate about other possible causes for the progress reported. As social workers and advocates we must be clear on *why* we are working on a problem, *what* it is we hope to achieve, *how* we plan to accomplish it, *who* will be the potential beneficiaries— and we can take responsibility for the results, whether secured in a solo or coalition effort.

One thing is certain: The family service board will not wonder if it should devote time to advocacy. Board members will be too busy with the question of how to move fast enough to help produce productive citizens in our minority population as an immediate community service to all people.

Before an agency can begin to do things to benefit others, many questions will be raised and answers must be found. Someone will inevitably wonder if advocacy activities will cause them difficulty with the tax exemption law. If an agency is involved in partisan politics, its tax-exempt status is undoubtedly in jeopardy. If it is involved in bringing services and opportunities, and in eradicating inequities based on race, color, or religion, it should not be difficult to assume an advocate stance and defend one's right to continue to do this by any means necessary. One thing an advocate cannot do: become the instrument of the funding source. A beginning advocate role for all people-oriented agencies is to make that fact known to foundations and funding establishments. By the same token, an advocate or advocate agency should not confuse the necessity of being politic with involvement in partisan politics. To be politic is to be wise in policy, tactful, expedient, shrewd, knowledgeable about government—all of which are strategies in living and in doing advocacy.

Unfortunately, *for whom* advocacy is done usually determines if an agency is acting within or outside of the law. In defining our right to serve all people and to use advocacy wherever appropriate, we must keep our eyes and ears open to spot double interpretations of the law based on the constituency to be served. If fighting air pollution is funded by the federal government and private sources, it is reasonable to expect no difficulty if an agency fights lack of garbage collection, destruction of natural resources due to overcrowded living conditions, and other common occurrences in low-income neighborhoods which contribute to air, water, and land pollution.

> The longer we wait and equivocate, the more surely are we setting policy by default, because this accelerated world will not wait for us. The problems demand full attention, full discussion, an effort towards agreement, and ultimate—hopefully *early*—action.[1]

Agency board members should begin to talk like Bayard Ewing, volunteer president of United Community Funds and Councils:

> The hour is very late in our cities. We must redeploy our dollars and our volunteer efforts. One critical way the United Way movement can be of particular help in the urban crisis is to provide seed money for innovative and experimental service programs aimed at helping the poor. We must put funds into innovative services to combat the ills of our society and help those who are unemployed or underemployed and those who suffer from drug addiction. But United Funds must obtain the advice of the poor in planning programs. They know their own needs far more than we do.[2]

Agency board members should also begin to watch the actions of William Aramony, newly appointed executive director of the United Community Funds and Councils, to help him insure that his words are the foundation from which he acts. Mr. Aramony has stated:

> To justify community support, the United Way must project a service umbrella that makes services available to all the people. And I stress all the people. The United Way movement must be an instrument to unify the community, not divide. It must be relevant to the needs of the people today, not as they were five or ten years ago. It must be community-oriented and service delivery-oriented, not agency-oriented. It must have powerful, representative boards led by the most influential people—industry influential, labor and business influential, and also poor influential. And it must be a major contributor to the community's ability to meet rapidly changing social conditions, not a party to forces that resist change.[3]

Finally, every board member should see the task of eradicating white racism and institutional racism as a personal responsibility to self and to the objectives of the agency. Ways to initiate meaningful avenues to eliminate racism are encounter workshops (known to FSAA as the Princeton Workshop); using the play *The Man Nobody Saw* at conferences, private affairs, and fund-raising appeals; and through orientation sessions of new and old board members. These approaches are advocacy and they hold hope of bringing about effective change.

Notes

1. Donald B. Hurwitz, Sectarian Services in the Crossfire of Current Problems, *Journal of Jewish Communal Service*, 46:296 (June 1970).

2. *Channels*, 22:1 (May 1, 1970).

3. *Channels*, 22:1 (May 1, 1970).

THE ROLE OF THE AGENCY BOARD AS ADVOCATE FOR CHILDREN

Mrs. Irwin C. Lieb

Although my topic is the role of the agency board as advocate for children, I can't help including advocacy for people of all ages. My association with the Child and Family Service of Austin naturally encourages me to see the child as a product of his family and his community environment; and so intricately involved in his makeup are these surrounding factors that efforts for the individual child must surely include efforts on behalf of his family and community. Indeed, we are always working for our children when we set out to challenge an injustice or improve our way of life, for without the prospect of the next generation and generations following, we would hardly feel enthusiasm for changing anything.

Consider the current ecological efforts which have garnered national recognition and support. Would we involve ourselves in such expensive and time-consuming enterprises if our aims were selfishly centered on our own life spans? No, we are trying to create a world which is better for our children and their children, but we are starting from where we are now—with our own generation—for it is the world as it exists now which is affecting and infecting our children.

So, indeed, the advocate, the defender, the pleader of causes, the supportive authority in each of us is always at work for the child, for our children, while it is at work for any improvement in the human condition.

All right. I am an adult. I have some authority, and I certainly do want the human condition improved. But I'm a very busy man, or I'm a "fragmented" housewife, and after all, I do sit on boards, attend PTA meetings, vote in elections, and contribute to charities—what else can I do? I'm not a professionally trained social worker. Isn't it enough that I help make it possible for social agencies to operate smoothly, so that others, who are professionally trained, can attend to the destructive forces in the community?

Without in the least diminishing the value of this service (that is, making the conditions for professional agencies to operate efficiently), there is a more active role we board members can take. We are beginning to have a sense of the real value of the combined effort, professional with non-professional, and it is heartening to see it at work.

But we must start where we are. For board members of social agencies whose intent is generous, though their time is limited, I would like to suggest there are many ways to serve as effective advocates, without specialized training. One of the most important ways to serve is readily available to all of us.

Each of us will sit, at some time or other, on the membership committee of his board. A very serious and ongoing problem of any board is just what should the board be? Should its membership be drawn from the influential and wealthy of the community, as has been the case traditionally? Particularly if we are talking of advocacy, influential boards are going to have more success working on behalf of those people who suffer most from racism, poverty, and legal injustice, than their less prominent cousins. And, money is not the root of all evil. It buys services and breeds more money for more beneficial services. No one questions the need for money and influence, but we have grown increasingly skeptical of boards made up entirely from this segment of the community. The monied and powerful are generally cut off from those very areas of the community which the agency most needs to serve. But what then is a balanced board? If we include the so-called indigenous or target area board members, how far do we carry this? Do we sacrifice board influence in the community, pressure on the sources of funding and city government legislation in the name of a balanced board? It is not easy to give up influence, as the agency's very position in the community is surely affected by this. Yet we know that the board has to be aware of the needs of the residents of target areas before it can establish priorities and policies for its agency.

Do we, then, keep our traditional board membership and ask target area residents to come to lunch with us once every three months and advise us on conditions (much like a local weather report), but not vote on policy? Advisory adjuncts to the board may be useful to the board, but these positions are certainly demeaning to its fringe members. Furthermore, finding articulate spokesmen from target areas, who are comfortable with establishment board members, or indeed even have time to come for lunch, is not an easy proposition. What then is the answer? Well, of course, there is not one answer. Each agency's membership committee will have to thrash this out for itself. One suggestion might be to hire paid consultants from poverty groups, or perhaps make better use of minority group paraprofessionals within the agency setting. In our case that would be our homemakers, and we are making a concerted effort to do this now.

In Austin the most blatantly needy areas in the community have been the ghettos of black and Mexican Americans. The Child and Family Service Board has excellent black and Mexican-American representation, but not indeed from the poverty areas. We have yet to solve this problem, frankly, though considerable thought has gone into the matter. Our board members, to a man, are from comfortable homes and successful positions.

We have succeeded, though, in turning the problem around. We were not able to find target area personnel to sit with us, so we went out and sat with them. A prime example, and a source of great pride for us, has been in our Becker Neighborhood Project. Here, very briefly, is some background on the Becker neighborhood, which surrounds a federal housing project. It serves to illustrate what can happen if board members join with professional staff in reaching out to where the problems are. The Child and Family Service undertook this project for two reasons: one, to teach ourselves how to be supportive of a neighborhood participation program and, two, because the area in question was virtually isolated from community support.

A neighborhood council was formed which included civic and church leaders, school, recreation, and welfare personnel, and area residents. Among the results then obtained were jobs for the male residents; summer employment for the youth; tutoring and counseling for the children; school clothing made available; a park site purchased; land cleared for a supervised playground; a multiservice center opened and staffed by Department of Public Welfare, Mental Health-Mental Retardation, and Child and Family Service personnel; a food distribution program improved; adult education, vocational training and job placement programs begun; tenants' councils formed to ease tensions and establish rules of fair play among the residents (who incidentally were not from minority groups); and other supportive projects, not the least of which is a court case now pending concerning the paving of streets in the area. Consultation on broadening neighborhood participation and organizing leadership in the community is ongoing.

This is the purest case of advocacy I can offer from our agency, as all of the destructive environmental forces which were bearing down on these low-income families were attacked where they were, and before the individual residents of the project sought our agency's caseworkers for individual counseling.

Now, let us back up for a minute. Impressive as this record is, it is not a record of board member advocacy for the child. Obviously, much of this project was carried out by the professional staff of our agency and by members of other established institutions in Austin. But the point is, members of our board were a necessary and active part of this project. It was board members who made contacts with the city council and HUD, it is board members who are pressing the law suit on behalf of the block clubs for street paving. Board members worked to establish the funding for this project and are now tackling the more desperate problem of the project's refunding. Board members worked with the staff throughout this program helping to open communication lines, to deal with the park issue, and to press the commodities distribution issue. For the power structure in any city lends an ear more quickly to established leaders in the community than to residents of the local area under consideration. That may be an unpleasant fact, but nonetheless it has to be reckoned with.

The Becker Neighborhood Project is but one project in which board members have taken a strong role in supporting the professional staff in its advocacy of people in need. Other less clear-cut examples could be cited. We now have board members actively supporting the school system in its plans to develop experimental programs in the black neighborhoods in Austin (though this project is in jeopardy now and will need some even stronger commitment to advocacy on the part of our board to see it through); our board members have recently established the FSAA Plays for Living project in Austin; board members have built up the funding for homemaker service, very definitely an advocacy program for people of all ages. Every time a board member goes to the sources of funding to plead for a budget commensurate with the needs of the staff to carry out its work in the community he is acting, though indirectly, as an advocate for people in need. Every time a board member interprets to the community current approaches to such ticklish subjects as drugs and abortions he is acting as an advocate.

What I am most anxious to convey, though, is that those of us who are nonprofessionals can assume roles in the community which surely come under the heading of advocacy. We decide who sits on our boards through constant review of the needs of the agency and of the skills required to support those projects which we, also as board members, have selected as priorities for our agency. We can make forays into the world outside of the board room, and we can learn something from the people out there. Perhaps we learn that the traditional approaches are not working, perhaps we learn that we do not know enough about the needs of people who do not actively seek our agencies, or perhaps, more cheerfully, we will learn that some of the most discouraged and hopeless groups of people in need in our cities are actually taking some heart from seeing us out in their world. But, I hasten to add, here lies a grave pitfall. Never must we give hope to people who are already inclined to distrust us, and then fail to follow through, or we will be guilty of irrevocably destroying the very goal we had hoped to achieve.

Recently our agency has been taking a long hard look at itself. In the board room we had all agreed that advocacy, as an idea, was a worthy approach. But under the scrutiny of a self-evaluation, we discovered that, for instance, the issue of including target area representatives on our board had not been settled. We could all agree that we needed the advice of the people we were trying to serve, but we have yet to agree quite how to achieve this end, though we have watched in wonder the enormously valuable lessons which could be learned from going out to the people in the Becker Neighborhood Project. From this experience and others, we decided to press our education further and have applied for a small grant from a foundation to study in depth just who it is we have been serving, as well as whom we have failed to serve.

Although it is our professional staff who is actually compiling the statistics for this internal evaluation, the board is being informed of the results, through a committee whose job it is to make recommendations to the board for action. As we had suspected, we are learning there are whole groups of people in need in Austin who are not making full use of the Child and Family Service. The blacks and Mexican Americans in Austin are comfortable with some of our resources, but such things as making and keeping appointments, coming to an agency building, talking with counselors, making long-range plans, and using phone contacts are more difficult for these groups than for other groups in Austin. Furthermore, we are failing to see enough of the newcomers to Austin who settle in outlying developments and whose problems of relocation and loneliness must surely be straining family relationships. We are beginning to sense that if we are to be responsive advocates for people in need, we will have to challenge even the very idea of a centrally located agency, as well as some of our traditional thinking about what a family is.

Advocacy requires reaching out to where the problems exist. If people in need are not finding you, you must be willing to go out and find them. And it is those of us who sit on agency boards who are in the position of lending professional staffs the flexibility needed to reach out.

We must be willing to make it clear to our professional staffs that we are totally committed to advocacy by developing new systems of evaluating staff time. Traditional toting-up of individual caseloads will no longer be a viable way of recognizing the efforts of staff members, for once embarked on a program of advocacy, agency time will be used in radically new ways. Each agency will have to reorganize its programs and services, and therefore its financial priorities, to make room for the larger reach of advocacy, and we must be prepared actively to seek recruitment of staff specially trained in advocacy method. It is not a time for the comfortable or cowardly, as advocacy forces upheavals in whole sets of systems and many community toes will be stepped on. But we cannot ask social workers to stick their necks out without being fully prepared to back them up, indeed stand with them, always cognizant of the jeopardy these actions may force.

Board members remain nonprofessional, but we must educate ourselves in the new methods of advocacy. And one of the best ways to get that education (busy business-men and fragmented housewives all) is to go ahead and step into that breach between the indigenous leadership and their professional counselors and the rigidity of established institutions. For every court case won, every street paved, every park site saved, every injustice challenged is, indeed, advocacy for the child, for our children, and our children's children!

CALLING IT ADVOCACY DOES NOT MAKE IT SO

S. Frances Brisbane

Mere employment of nonprofessionals does not make them instant family advocates. An outpost or outreach office is not necessarily an advocate agency. Many agencies have employed community aides, case assistants, paraprofessionals, detached workers and team assistants. Workers serving under these titles while performing a multitude of services are not necessarily fulfilling the role of an advocate. In order for their employment to be meaningful and in the spirit and design of advocacy, the following must be clearly defined and vigorously implemented: job description, defining area of job responsibility; job training; salary scale; promotional opportunities; criteria for advancement; fringe benefits; and opportunities for higher education.

Too long have we assumed wrongly the following about the indigenous employee and ghetto communities:

1. He is expected to have natural, immediate rapport with his ghetto neighbors.

2. He can automatically communicate well with all people of his socioeconomic background, understand the problems of oppression, poverty, and exploitation, and confirm

the agency's hope that entering into dialogue with the poor about these conditions is meaningful and curative in nature. 3. He should work long hours and take great risks to help his neighbor without the expectation of adequate wages, and without any outward signs of a desire for self-fulfillment and upward mobility. 4. The ghetto is a community with geographical boundaries containing many people who are judged to be the same by outsiders. Residents are characterized by their weaknesses as a group. The outsider is blinded to the individual strengths. Individuals are without self-identity and work, a part of a seeking, faceless mass.

The agency should never be guilty of creating a position which locks an indigenous worker into poverty. If no avenues are opened for advancement through training grants, released time, or the equivalent, the job is a vicious cycle of dependency which creates a sense of worthlessness and possible loss of ability to identify with the agency's total purpose. If the only available employment of a noncredentialed worker without a college degree is in a subservient, nonpromotional category, great consideration should be given to the development of intermediary career-level advancement. If indigenous people are employed in any number and adequate provisions are not made for their own individual and professional development, the agency may only be fulfilling its own manpower requirement.

An agency that has an employee—professional or nonprofessional—assigned to an outpost, or has an indigenous detached worker, must take the initiative and responsibility of making the employment meaningful and connected to the total agency service. These employees must receive necessary training and interaction with other staff members in order to better serve both the agency and the community. Creating a job for or giving a job to a person and leaving him on his own may be a total disservice to individual, agency, and community. With particular reference to the indigenous detached worker, he must never feel detached from the agency. The function which the agency feels is the reason for establishing an outpost should determine the qualifications of the person employed. All too frequently the agency hires indigenous people or releases a professional to serve in an outpost and the function of the outpost conforms to their abilities, not to community need.

The outpost which does not touch the lives of people may be too steeped in professionalism. If so, the same obstacles to people's utilization of service are repeated at a "closer distance." It is usually not the great distance from the main office which keeps most low-income people or minority group members from using the agency service. Therefore, the model and design of the outpost should pattern itself after the needs and life-styles of the people. These are basic prerequisites for an outpost to become an advocate agency.

SOCIAL ADVOCACY: A NEW DIMENSION IN SOCIAL WORK

Mary J. McCormick

The dimensions of social work are difficult to identify. They appear to shift and change, not only with changing times but with every refinement of the knowledge, understanding, and skill that characterize professional performance. Length, depth, and breadth take on new and different meanings whenever, for example, goal and purpose are reexamined or redefined; they bring new and different challenges whenever basic values are probed or established responsibilities are questioned. Perhaps this is one reason why the present commitment to *advocacy* as an objective (in contrast to *reform* in the early 1900s and *therapy* in more recent years) gives rise to concern, and even consternation, among those for whom reason and discipline, rather than feeling and emotion, direct professional activity. From this vantage point, the apparent abandonment of familiar structure and methodology appears to be a potentially destructive factor in social work at the threshold of the 1970s. The realization

---

Reprinted from *Social Casework*, January 1970.

that this same factor is exerting similar, and sometimes more drastic, influence on law, medicine, education, and the ministry does not dispel the anxiety that is so often aroused by innovation and experimentation.

There is, however, another vantage point from which the situation can be viewed, namely, *social change.* Within this sociological framework, the new and the untried can be appraised, first in the light of the circumstances that spark the desire for change and then in the thought and action of those who assume responsibility for making that desire a reality. In this continuum of cause and effect, with its judgment on *what should be* as well as *what is,* the new and the old assume complementary roles and together offer a rationale for what is to follow. Change per se is then placed in its true perspective as a normal, anticipated factor in the realization of social progress and individual well-being.

In his article, "Changing Theory and Changing Practice," Charles Grosser elaborates on this historical perspective. He points out that, in the progress of every social movement:

> . . . there comes a time when theories, methods, ideologies, and technologies developed in an earlier period must be modified, more or less drastically, to suit changed circumstances. . . . Ultimately a new entity emerges, which while retaining features from the past, incorporates substantial innovation.[1]

If the advocacy concept follows this pattern and retains the strengths of the past while shaping the innovations of the present, then social work should not be in jeopardy. If, on the contrary, an overly enthusiastic acceptance of the new diminishes the import of the old, the fears of the skeptics could be realized.

In the face of this contingency, it seems worthwhile to explore the concept of advocacy within the total context of the helping process and to evaluate it against man's desire for, and implementation of, planned change. Both the desire and the fulfillment are reflected in the objectives of social work as these have evolved over the years—from the reform of the pioneers, with their reliance on social conscience, to the therapy of the clinicians and their focus on the individual unconscious. Against this background, advocacy, with its unreserved commitment to the "plight of the disadvantaged," [2] stands out in bold relief; it adds a new dimension, that of *breadth*, to the objectives of the social work of the future.

Perhaps because this dimension is essentially political-social in nature, it seems more akin to revolution than to evolution; hence the fears that it engenders. The anxiety reaction is likely to persist, in varying degrees, until such time as advocacy in the abstract (in its conceptual meaning) is internalized, that is, until it becomes an integral part of the structure and function of social work and of the basic convictions of social workers—administrators, educators, and practitioners alike. Only then will advocacy, in the concrete, be recognized as an acceptable, professional objective, grounded in a social structure that, according to Talcott Parsons, makes possible the legitimation of political-social action. It is in this process of legitimation, when personal ideas and ideals become absorbed into the social system (become institutionalized), that advocacy—as idea and ideal —will find justification and support within the structure of social work at the professional level.[3]

The idea and the ideal

The concept of advocacy has long been associated, in its general meaning, with the defense or promotion of a cause and, more specifically, with pleading the cause of another. In the first instance, the activities are political-social in character; in the second, they can be described more accurately as personal-social. In the political context, the objective is to bring active support to ideas and programs that will benefit society as a whole, as well as particular segments of it. Extent and breadth are important, both to the cause and its promulgation. In the second context, the focus is on the individual in his relations with other individuals and institutions: employer or landlord, court of law or welfare agency. In both contexts, the advocate, whether legislator or lawyer, social worker or health officer, "is, in fact, a partisan in a social conflict, and his expertise is available exclusively to serve client interests." [4] This is the advocate's role, whether the client is one person or one family, an entire community, group, or nation. It reflects the sweeping changes that, by the late sixties, have taken place in society at large and that are, at the approach to the seventies, exerting their influence on the helping professions.

The nature of such a role and the responsibilities attached to it were recognized half a century ago by the leaders of what was then an emerging profession. For Jane Addams and Mary Richmond (to mention the familiar names) "direct engagement with the problems of the poor" [5]—wording that Grosser used in 1965—was already a way of life. For Robert Kelso, it was the "historical rootstock of social work." [6] In his presidential address to the National Conference of Social Work in 1922, Kelso accorded this "engagement" the dual status of social philosophy and historical fact. To him, "the most far-reaching change in American history" was also the "basic fact" in American social work, namely, ". . . *social relationship* [was made] *the basis of our law, and social necessity the driving force in its development.*" The process of analyzing the relationship and identifying the necessity was called social work. The objective, both of the change and the process, was "to achieve the greatest benefit to the greatest number at the least sacrifice to person and to property." To carry out the process and realize the objective, it was, in turn, necessary to have "an analyst of our social contacts, a professional student of human relations, a statesman to shape our social thinking. So enters the trained social worker." [7]

The rationale and the description both of social work and social worker may seem, on first reading, to belong to a distant and outmoded past, and yet both were, in effect, revived in 1964 by the National Association of Social Workers Commission on Social Work Practice when it formulated the "Working Definition of Social Work Practice." The commission, charged with the responsibility to clarify the nature of practice, developed the "social-worker-in-action" concept and, to quote Harriett Bartlett, identified it as the "core" of professional practice. In Bartlett's words, "In the last analysis, it is the worker's action that makes a difference, if any change is to take place, in the events and situations with which social work is concerned." [8] The connecting link between the thoughts expressed by Kelso in 1922 and by Bartlett in 1964 seems fairly obvious; it is the link of *democracy*. According to John Kidneigh, social work, during these forty years, has come more and more "to be a conscious application of democratic principles with an increasing understanding of the dynamics of human behavior and of the social process." [9] Consequently:

> As an integral part of a dynamic and changing society, the profession of social work in America continues to be concerned with people, how they fare as the nations grow, develop, and change, and how they might fare better. [10]

It seems logical to find in Kelso's and Kidneigh's statements —each of which incorporates the ideas and ideals of a democratic social order—the conceptual base for advocacy, both in its political-social and personal-social manifestations.

Clarification of this base calls for an exploration of advocacy as an instrument of social action within the context, first, of the democratic process and then of the helping process. In the first instance, advocacy is viewed as a planned and directed operation, accepted on its own merits and, in the light of history, as an effective means of initiating or supporting a *cause*. In the second instance, the focus shifts to the role and use of that instrument within the traditional structure of American social work, the casework, group work, or community organization within which the helping process takes place.

Advocacy and social action

"Social action is the business of social work"; [11] advocacy is an instrument of social action. As such, it brings the dimension of breadth or largeness to plans and programs directed toward change and, at the same time, supplies the vitality and dedication that are important assets. Success, however, depends on something more than these contributions of mind and heart; it requires "an understanding of the methods by which change occurs and an awareness of the political process in which it unfolds." [12] The first of these requirements is formidable and calls for a deeper exploration than can be undertaken here.

The second requirement (awareness of political process), however, lends itself to discussion at a different level of abstraction. This is fortunate, since the political aspects of advocacy, in its adaption to professional practice, raise strategic, and sometimes disquieting, issues. It seems reasonable to assume that the disquietude prevails, to greater or lesser degree, both among the traditionalists, who are committed to the structure (of social work) that has been developed over the years, and among the more liberal-minded, who are disillusioned by that structure. Followers of both persuasions will very likely agree that, in an era of rapid change, the real test of a profession is its ability to meet constructively the demands of that change. However, they will disagree about the quality and quantity, the character and extent of change and, most of all, about the controls to which it could, or should, be subjected. Must change be supported unconditionally? Should advocacy as an instrument be left unhampered, or should guidelines be set and limits imposed?

Answers to these questions are difficult to formulate. They revolve around the importance attached to such factors as ethical codes, objective judgments, decision-making based on scientific knowledge, skill in problem-solving, and the proper use of authority; in short, they are intimately associated with the criteria of a profession. This means that the professional person, as he contemplates the political aspects of advocacy, must make the comparison, and mark the contrast, between the *professional* approach, which is grounded in the past and judged by some to be irrelevant to the present, and the *political* approach, which, in its identification with the democratic process, is also grounded in the past but is judged by many to be wholly relevant. This latter opinion is most likely shaped by the fact that political activity focuses on the present and the future, on how things are and how they ought to be. There is in it that crusading zeal that is so much a part of the American temperament, a zeal that would have the "better" of the future replace without delay the "good" (or the "bad") of the present.

In pursuing its objectives, whether long or short range, political-social action admits and often relies on practices that have traditionally been anathema to the professions. For example, such action not only approves but encourages the manipulation that George Brager (quoting Richard Christie) describes as "the use of guile in interpersonal relations." [13] This manipulation permits and sometimes makes mandatory a highly partisan representation of interests that rules out opposing positions per se. Its thrust depends on total commitment to a cause and, in the interest of that commitment, to the development of "the most effective case . . . rather than the most complete or reasoned one." [14] This opens the way for that artfulness that is implied in the root meaning of *politic* and that Brager describes as "the conscious rearranging of reality to induce a desired attitudinal or behavioral outcome." [15]

This reference to the characteristics of advocacy in its political-social context is not intended as criticism. The intent, rather, is to examine what seems to be its core technique: manipulation as it relates to the social action that is social work and in turn influences the social-worker-in-action.

Brager makes a case for manipulation as an instrument that social work and social workers are, and have been, using. This use may occur in "response to the social climate" [16] or to what Grosser calls social work's " 'agonizing reappraisal' " [17] of itself. Whatever the motivation, the role thus created is a strategic one since it "inevitably requires that the practitioner function as a political tactician." As such, his primary responsibiliy is "the tough-minded and partisan representation" of the interests of the "disadvantaged" segment of the population, a responsibility that, within this context, "supersedes" all others.[18]

Brager examines the dynamics of this "political" role and applies his findings to three "professional approaches" that he considers to be characteristic of social work, namely, process orientation, clinical orientation, and social reform. He describes the first of these as distinct from the others "in that process is valued for its own sake." The process-oriented worker "feels little pressure to influence the attitudes or behavior of others" and therefore is likely to be less manipulative than the others. The clinical worker, however, seeks improved functioning through changes in personality, attitudes, or behavior and is likely "to engage in manipulative activity." Brager adds that if Christie is correct, "the formal role of the clinician makes this inevitable." In sharp contrast to both of these, the third approach (reform) "seeks to make an impact on social problems by influencing change in organizations and institutions." In line with this objective, advocacy "*must* be a part of the worker's armamentarium" and "the reformer is more likely to embrace this activity than are his professional colleagues." [19]

Regardless of these differences—whether in orientation, objectives, or methodology—social work, as it functions within the professional frame of reference, does have a common denominator, namely, a code of ethics. The preamble to that code emphasizes "service for the welfare of mankind"; it identifies practice as a "public trust" that "requires . . . integrity, compassion, belief in the dignity and worth of human beings, and a dedication to truth." The code itself spells out these responsibilities as they encompass the social worker's "relationships with those he serves, with his colleagues, with his employing agency, with other professions, and with the community." [20] The wording is interesting in its scope and sequence. It can be interpreted *either* as giving definite priority to those who are served *or* as attaching equal importance to colleagues, agencies, and communities. If this latter interpretation is accepted, then the scope of responsibility is broadened and the principles of the code apply, with like sanction, to each of the designated groups.

This either-or factor is, perhaps, the crux of the potential conflict that exists between political-social action and professional action. Certainly, as Daniel Thursz points out, the "social work profession cannot allow its preoccupation with status and with the acquisition of various professional attributes or artifacts to hinder its full commitment to social action and social reform." [21] But neither can social work, or any other profession, become engulfed in total commitment to one group if, in doing so, it violates or ignores the positions rightfully held by other groups, whether welfare agencies or educational institutions, standard-setting organizations, or community planners.

The dilemma thus created is recognized in the report of the NASW Ad Hoc Committee on Advocacy, which mentions specifically the "possibility that in promoting his clients' interests the social worker may be injuring other aggrieved persons with an equally just claim." It suggests that in this situation "professional norms would appear to dictate" that such claims not be pressed "in a partisan manner"; on the contrary, the professional person should "seek to weigh the relative urgency" of such claims. [22] The operative word is *relative*; diverse issues must be balanced within a total situation, and their relationship to each other must be weighed in that balance. The importance of this suggestion is that it places some reliance on a professional code, even though such a code can deal with principles and practices only in their broadest possible implications; it cannot fit them to specific cases.

This absence of specificity means that, for the present and perhaps the immediate future, the answers to the questions surrounding partisanship, and therefore manipulation, can be found only in the principle of personal responsibility. This is the all-important principle that is grounded in the personally responsible intellectual activity that Abraham Flexner designated as "the first mark of a profession." In Flexner's judgment, "This quality of responsibility follows from the fact that . . . the thinker takes upon himself a risk," the kind of risk that is inevitable in strategic decision-making. In assuming this risk, the professional person "exercises a very large discretion as to what he shall do." [23] Perhaps this is the discretion that must be exercised by the social worker when "what he shall do" involves political social advocacy.[24]

Advocacy and the helping process

Within the framework of the helping professions, the concept of advocacy is generally associated with the law and, therefore, with the "social relationship" that Kelso accepted as the basis of the legal system. As an instrument of this system, it is the duty of the advocate (lawyer) "to represent his client zealously within the bounds of the law." [25] His "professional judgment" is to be exercised within these bounds "solely for the benefit of his client and free of compromising influences and loyalties." [26] His obligations, as formulated in the Code of Professional Responsibility, extend "to the public, to the legal system and to the legal profession." [27] Failure to meet these obligations, whether through omission or commission, carries definite sanction. It leads to the enforcement—by the profession itself, by agencies of government, or both—of disciplinary measures that are supported by the rule of law and by a society that respects this rule.

In Kelso's thinking, this social relationship was not only the basis of law; it was the "basic fact" of social work, that is, of a helping profession that relies on the helping process. In this process, the duty of the advocate (the social worker) extends beyond representation of a client within established boundaries; it calls for involvement with a client in a multi-faceted situation that is sociopsychological in character and therefore highly complex. Gordon Hamilton expressed the complexity when she wrote: "Social work is, perhaps, the only profession in which involvement of the whole person within the whole situation is the goal and process." [28] The goal may be social betterment or personal development. The process calls for intervention in the literal meaning of "interference that may affect the interests of others." [29] Since advocacy is a form of interference, it finds its place, quite logically, among the responsibilities of a profession committed to the kind of involvement that sets in motion the helping process and directs it toward "the all-encompassing central goal and aspiration of social work," namely, "service for the welfare of mankind." [30]

At the performance level, this goal is defined more specifically by the particular methods that social work claims as its own: casework, group work, and community organization. It is at this level also that methods and process are consolidated in a particular kind of association, namely, the professional relationship. Once this is established the social worker is able to participate constructively in the life experiences of other persons, either as individuals or as members of a community. In the course of his participation, he comes face to face with the challenge of advocacy in its role and its use. In this confrontation, the social-worker-in-action must make his own judgment, to his own professional satisfaction, about the role of advocacy in the helping process and the validity of its use in the service of human beings. [31]

There is no attempt, within the limits of this presentation, to elaborate on the first aspect of such a challenge, since the role of advocacy, as currently defined, seems clear enough; it is the defense of, or the promotion of, a *cause*. In the resulting activity, social work may speak alone as the responsible advocate, or it may join forces with other professions and groups. In either event, its role has been explored with considerable acumen by such authorities as Brager, Thursz, Briar, Epstein, and Grosser, and its relationship to practice has been examined by the Ad Hoc Committee on Advocacy.[32] In a less direct manner, and without using the word advocacy, John Turner has described its extent and breadth in terms of the "front-line institutional functions that are required to produce and to maintain a socially productive man in a humanized society."[33] Advocacy is surely one such function.

In his article, "Social Work at the Crossroad," Turner contends that the future of the profession depends on the path that it chooses to follow during these critical years of change. There are two choices. One leads to diminished responsibility "for remedying human ills" by withdrawal into highly specialized areas of practice or restricted areas of a community.[34] The other leads to positive action in the interests of people and their problems by reaching out, if necessary "into the ghetto neighborhoods with store-front offices and an open door."[35] It means bringing services to people, whoever and wherever they are.

If social work follows the first course, its future can be jeopardized by activities that are out of touch with a society in which change is the order of the day. The point is a strategic one, for, as Turner sees it, the real test of a profession is its ability to be relevant to the problems that come within its area of competence. He points to this question of relevance as the "single most important question to be asked," both by the leaders who carry responsibility for the future of social work and by the clientele it is expected to serve.[36] Each group must somehow assess realistically the demands of a changing world and the needs of a changing people. Moreover, each must recognize and strive to adjust to the rapidity of that change and the pressures thus exerted, both on the profession and on those who look to it for action that is sound in principle and relevant in practice.

This is the kind of action that should result when social work gives equal consideration to objective facts about a problem and to practical proposals for its solution. Such consideration should make it possible for the social-worker-in-action to maintain a reasonable balance between the "expertise and methods of problem intervention" that characterize advocacy as a component of the helping process and the "substantive knowledge about social problems and their solutions" that is the hallmark of professional help. Turner's conclusion is applicable here:

> . . . if it [social work] can fuse its penchant for social action with expertise about deciding outcomes—then the profession will have indeed successfully met the test of being relevant to the human condition.[37]

It seems reasonable to assume that, once this fusion takes place, social work will be closer to meeting the test of advocacy, both as an instrument of social action and as part of the helping process.

It seems equally reasonable to assume that such a course will bring social workers face to face with additional problems of decision-making. The humanistic goals identified by the profession may require practitioners, administrators, and educators to engage in "forms of expression and action . . . that are often considered controversial." [38] Political advocacy and its technique of manipulation are cases in point. Currently, many professional persons accept the technique as an effective and valid approach to social issues; others look upon it as a flagrant violation of professional standards. The social worker who uses it may be praised or blamed; his status, professional and economic, may be threatened or enhanced. Whatever the consequences, engagement in this or another controversial activity presupposes "firm dedication and deep conviction" [39] along with a keen sense of personal obligation. Otherwise the risk, which Flexner described as a mark of professionalism, would not be taken. In reality, it is taken in one form or another whenever a professional man or woman believes that human welfare is threatened and that his involvement will somehow alleviate or remove that threat.[40]

Commitment like this is serious, demanding, and often frustrating. The social worker who makes it does so knowing that "neither the profession, . . . nor any of its methods singly or in combination, has the knowledge or power" to deal conclusively with the issues at stake.[41] There must be an additional dimension. Currently, that dimension seems to be advocacy, both as concept and as instrument. Conceptually, such a dimension represents the ideas and ideals of a democratic social order and of social work as a profession; instrumentally, it exerts forceful influence on what happens, both in the order and in the profession.

If advocacy is accepted as a plus value in the helping process, then it should be distinguished in a positive manner from the more familiar political and legal forms. This distinction is to be found in the social character of the advocacy that focuses on "the whole person within the whole situation" [42] and finds its orientation in substantive knowledge about the complexities of human nature and the pressures, external and internal, to which human beings are subjected. In the attempts to remove or alleviate these pressures, social advocacy as an instrument of social work is identifiable by the objective consideration that it gives to means and to ends, to the ways in which its goals are approached, as well as to the goals themselves. It seems reasonable to expect that, as the concept is developed and the instrument refined, this consideration will extend to the formal structure of social work as well as to its professional practices. The principles and values of social work as it has evolved over the years will be recognized and respected by those who are committed to advocacy as a challenging technique and a new dimension.

This concurrence with certain aspects of established structure and principles does not, in any way, preclude rational attempts to change the structure and reassess the principles. Turner believes that such change is mandatory if social work is to function with relevance in today's world.[43] Thursz underscores the belief when he points out that the reappraisal of principles is a professional charge that cannot, in honesty, be evaded.[44] Responsibility for implementing such examination and change rests with equal sanction on those who maintain a basic loyalty to the old and those who are enthusiastically committed to the new. In the last analysis, each must be willing to learn from the other and to act in accordance with that learning. This kind of reconciliation is always challenging insofar as neither party can afford to violate its own fundamental convictions or relinquish its own identity.

The balance is not easy to achieve, but social work is not inexperienced in such an achievement. More than thirty years ago, Gordon Hamilton, in her analysis of the basic concepts of casework, concluded that "the ultimate issue of our day is to develop greater capacity to think and act with others without losing the capacity to think and act for ourselves." [45] It would seem that the "ultimate issue" of 1937 finds its counterpart today. It seems, too, that the issue can be resolved only when social workers, irrespective of individual differences, are at long last capable of thinking and acting with the integrity, competence, and dedication to trust that symbolize the idea and the ideal of "service for the welfare of mankind."

Notes

1. Charles F. Grosser, Changing Theory and Changing Practice, *Social Casework*, 50:16 (January 1969).

2. George A. Brager, Advocacy and Political Behavior, *Social Work*, 13:6 (April 1968).

3. Talcott Parsons, An Outline of the Social System, in Talcott Parsons et al., eds., *Theories of Society: Foundations of Modern Sociological Theory*, 1:43–45 (New York: The Free Press of Glencoe, 1961).

4. Charles F. Grosser, Community Development Programs Serving the Urban Poor, *Social Work*, 10:18 (July 1965).

5. Ibid., p. 16.

6. Robert W. Kelso, Changing Fundamentals of Social Work, in Fern Lowry, ed., *Readings in Social Case Work, 1920–1938* (New York: Columbia University Press, 1939), p. 6.

7. Ibid., pp. 5–6.

8. Harriett M. Bartlett, The Place and Use of Knowledge in Social Work Practice, *Social Work,* 9:36 (July 1964).

9. John C. Kidneigh, History of American Social Work, in Harry L. Lurie, ed., *Encyclopedia of Social Work* (New York: National Association of Social Workers, 1965), p. 11.

10. Ibid., p. 18.

11. Daniel Thursz, Social Action as a Professional Responsibility, *Social Work,* 11:13 (July 1966).

12. Ibid.

13. Brager, Advocacy and Political Behavior, p. 9.

14. Ibid., p. 10.

15. Ibid., p. 8.

16. Ibid., p. 5.

17. Grosser, Changing Theory, p. 16.

18. Brager, Advocacy and Political Behavior, p. 6.

19. Ibid., pp. 9–10.

20. NASW Code of Ethics (adopted by the Delegate Assembly of the National Association of Social Workers, October 13, 1960); reprinted in *NASW News,* 6:14 (February 1961).

21. Thursz, Social Action, p. 13.

22. The Ad Hoc Committee on Advocacy, The Social Worker as Advocate: Champion of Social Victims, *Social Work,* 14:19 (April 1969).

23. Abraham Flexner, Is Social Work a Profession?, in *Proceedings of the National Conference of Charities and Correction* (Chicago: The Hildmann Printing Company, 1915), p. 578.

24. Mary J. McCormick, Professional Codes and the Educational Process, *Journal of Education for Social Work,* 2:57–65 (Fall 1966).

25. Special Committee on Evaluation of Ethical Standards, American Bar Association, *Code of Professional Responsibility* (preliminary draft, January 15, 1969), Canon, 7 ¶ 1, p. 77.

26. Ibid., Canon 6, ¶ 1, p. 60.

27. Ibid., Preamble, p. 1.

28. Gordon Hamilton, The Role of Social Casework in Social Policy, in Cora Kasius, ed., *Social Casework in the Fifties* (New York: Family Service Association of America, 1962), p. 34.

29. *Webster's New International Dictionary*, 2nd ed., s.v. "intervention."

30. Committee on the Study of Competence, *Guidelines for the Assessment of Professional Practice in Social Work* (New York: National Association of Social Workers, 1968), p. 13

31. Mary J. McCormick, Professional Responsibility and the Professional Image, *Social Casework*, 47:635–42 (December 1966).

32. Brager, Advocacy and Political Behavior, pp. 5–15; Thursz, Social Action, pp. 12–21; Scott Briar, The Social Worker's Responsibility for the Rights of Clients, *New Perspectives*, 1:89–92 (Spring 1967); Irwin Epstein, Social Workers and Social Action: Attitudes Toward Social Action Strategies, *Social Work*, 13:101–8; and Grosser, Community Development Programs, pp. 15–21.

33. John B. Turner, In Response to Change: Social Work at the Crossroad, *Social Work*, 13:9 (July 1968).

34. Ibid., p. 15.

35. Lydia Rapoport, Social Casework: An Appraisal and an Affirmation, *Smith College Studies in Social Work*, 39:219 (June 1969).

36. Turner, In Response to Change, p. 7.

37. Ibid., p. 15.

38. Committee on the Study of Competence, *Guidelines*, p. 16.

39. Ibid., p. 13.

40. Ibid., p. 16.

41. Rapoport, Social Casework, p. 215.

42. Hamilton, The Role of Social Casework, p. 34.

43. Turner, In Response to Change, p. 7.

44. Thursz, Social Action.

45. Gordon Hamilton, Basic Concepts in Social Case Work, in Lowry, *Readings in Social Case Work, 1920–1938,* p. 171.

THE SOCIAL WORKER AS
AGENT OF POLICY CHANGE

Charles S. Levy

In an important sense, social work practice in general is a matter of shaping, selecting, or influencing policy. For the individual client or family or group with considerable competence or authority to manage their own affairs, this means assistance in sorting out needs, priorities, and preferences and in selecting alternatives calculated to provide for them. For the individual client or family or group lacking either competence or authority, this means helping or influencing those who act in their behalf so that the interests of all are acknowledged and provided for. For those individuals or groups whose fate rests on institutional or legislative choices, this means applying influence or pressure with the goal of establishing conditions most conducive to their well-being and development.

In each case, the social worker with professional responsibility is helping to establish the value premises and the preferences for action that relate to the client's (clients')

Reprinted from *Social Casework*, February 1970.

need.[1] In each case, however, the social worker must deal with forces not always—in fact, rarely—directly related to the need for action.

Problem of choices

For example, an individual client—even when he is sufficiently poised, despite his presenting problem, to engage in a learned intellectual exchange with the social worker and is sufficiently self-possessed to understand the reasons for his difficulties and the actions required to solve them—is often torn between choices that immobilize him or make his problem less manageable. If he resents his wife's behavior but is hard put to risk her disfavor, if he cannot tolerate his son's willfulness but dreads the prospect of complete and final rebellion, if he feels oppressed by his parents' excessive watchfulness but dares not incur their wrath because of his dependence upon them, the social worker will be challenged to assist him in selecting and acting upon one set of choices that will help him to cope with the problems that discomfort or deprive him. The social worker's practice with the client, then, is based upon the identification of the client's difficulty, the determination of preferred approaches to dealing with it, and the generation of sufficient skill and conviction on the client's part to apply these approaches until the discomfort or deprivation is reduced or eliminated.

This procedure applies to practical, material problems as well as to psychological and social problems. The unemployed or economically unsuccessful husband who is absorbed in indignation over his wife's assumption of what he considers to be his legitimate function must either learn how to live with his plight or plot and act upon a course to escape it. He must take either step on the basis of his having previously decided whether or not to preserve his relationship with his wife. For the client to be helped by social work requires his appreciation of the part that social and psychological contributions play in his response to his situation, reckoning with the emotional as well as social consequences, discrimination between realistic and unrealistic plans of action, choosing a feasible plan, and skillful and intentional preparation for implementing it.

When a client is not so self-possessed or able, the resulting approach is not necessarily different. However, very different qualities of emotional reaction and different levels of self-awareness on the part of the client, as well as different degrees of initiative on the part of the social worker, are apt to be evident.

Something new is added when choices of interpretation of the client's problem and of approaches to its resolution are necessarily allocated to others—parents or guardians, for example. The social worker's practice, however, is no less focused on the formulation of what may be called a policy—that is, a system of value decisions to guide planning and action regarding an identified need or problem, such as a life plan, an income gap, a relationship, or a crisis.

Policy decisions affecting classes of people

Matters become much more complex when the social worker attempts to affect policy, either in its formulation or implementation, at levels beyond the client or family or group and beyond persons with a direct stake, jurisdiction, concern, or accountability for this client's status and welfare —at levels that affect classes of persons with whom the client and his problem are associated. Complexity of practice is increased by those factors inherent in the nature of the client's need or problem that would affect decisions about public assistance minima or guaranteed annual incomes in the face of a straining income tax structure and runaway inflation. However, a major reason for greater complexity in the social worker's practice at these levels is that those who purportedly make the policy decisions affecting large masses of persons like the social worker's clients are influenced by myriad forces, persons, values, and aspirations, not all of which relate directly to the policy decisions to be made. The more inclusive the scope of the policy and the range of persons, institutions, and governmental units that it affects, the more complex the practice problem becomes for the social worker who would presume to affect or influence policy, and the less amenable it becomes to his influence.

At this level of policy influence, one must deal not only with the personal and psychological influences acting upon participants in the policymaking process—although these, too, certainly are relevant—but also with their social and political aspirations and preoccupations. True, policymakers are not likely to be exempt from ideological remnants of their own various stages of development, including familial and reference group orientations with which the social worker may be confronted whether he is aware of them or not. In addition, participants in the policymaking process will be significantly affected by their wish to be reelected by their constituents or reappointed by the executive in charge. The social worker who would influence policymaking, therefore, whether to benefit specific clients or general classes of clientele, necessarily faces unwieldly targets and a multiplicity of adversaries.

Although this reality can hardly be used to discourage social work efforts in policy formulation or to suggest abandonment of professional educational objectives designed to develop students' skill in policy formulation, it ought to temper expectations in this realm, or at least to stimulate recognition of limitations so that provision may be made to cope with the situation realistically.

Multiple factors affecting policy decisions

Despite the validity of an emphasis on social policy in the educational preparation of social workers that was proposed by Eveline Burns in 1961 [2] and has been repeatedly urged ever since, there is something illusory about its productivity. To characterize as a responsibility of professional social work (even if only in part as the legitimate preoccupation of *some* social workers) the effecting of social policy at any level of appreciable influence on the lives and fates of classes of persons is to minimize the myriad influences on people who make policy and the myriad intervening variables that affect their participation in the policymaking process. It is not always possible to determine *who* or *what* really makes policy in agencies or in upper levels of governmental hierarchy. Nor is it possible to determine *whom* or *what* the social worker is supposed to influence in shaping policy in a preferred direction—for example, to help the poor, or blacks, or ghetto groups. It is insufficient to assume that the group of record in the policymaking process—whether an agency board, a community organization, or a legislative body—is the group of persons that actually makes the given policy, for that is rarely the case regardless of the prescribed procedure. The multiplicity of factors operating to effect expression of policy hardly makes the participants in the policymaking process amenable to the influence of the professional practitioner simply because he wills it. Work through a group of clients or other prospective beneficiaries might indeed have an impact on the participants, as recent events have graphically demonstrated, but this cannot be regarded as the consequence of applying a professional skill readily learned in a school of social work. Obviously, the higher the political or communal level of the policymaking involved, and the broader the range of persons affected by it, the less amenable to planned influence or change it is likely to be.

In fact, policymaking, especially at higher levels of government or community, is unwieldly, not only for a social worker who may seek to influence it directly or through mediating groups, but also for the very participants in the process, including leadership. William Gorham provides a realistic perspective of what may face anyone with sufficient daring or conviction to make the attempt:

To turn, first, to the political realities: Regard some of the difficulties facing the Secretary of Health, Education, and Welfare in designing a budget and legislative program which he seeks to measure in cost and benefit terms. Clearly, both the President and the Congress may have preferences about programs—preferences which may be unrelated to such costs and benefits. Congressional support may develop for a particular program because its beneficiaries are numerous, or are politically powerful or vocal. Or there are the accidental facts: the chairman of a relevant committee is interested in deaf children because he has one, or in cardiac research because he just had a heart attack. It may be easier to win passage of an increase in Social Security benefits, because such benefits are financed from a payroll tax, than for increases in Public Assistance, which must come out of general revenues. Similarly, it may be easier to get Congress to build highways out of the proceeds of the gasoline tax than to devote general revenues to building schools or hospitals.

This complex interplay of forces in Congress makes decision making in the Executive Branch a complicated game. The President must frame his budget in a fashion consistent with the state of the economy, and he must divide the total among Departments and Agencies. The Secretary of HEW must allocate his own portion among competing programs in his Department. But both the President and the Secretary are aware that they are not cutting a pie of known size. If the Executive Branch wants a large pie, it must guess accurately which programs the Congress will find most attractive [3]

Policy control and change

If, as Peter Drucker has suggested, "policy control by the political organs of government" might ever have been taken for granted, it certainly cannot be taken for granted today at the municipal level any more than at the national level, and not in the private sector any more than in the public sector, especially when these affect each other. "This growing disparity between apparent power and actual lack of control," Drucker adds, "is perhaps the greatest crisis of government."⁴ What is relevant for the existing political centers of "apparent power" must certainly be relevant for those who would presume to affect them. Their capacity to effect a policy that they prefer is necessarily limited, to say the least. It is hard enough, by professional design, to influence policymakers in chosen directions when they really carry policymaking authority; it must too often be impossible to influence policy when policymakers are more victims than perpetrators of policy. They may be making some decisions, but to what degree the decisions are theirs and how related they are to the merits of a given cause and the values by which they should be measured cannot readily be determined. Where, then, would the skill in social policymaking that the social worker is supposed to be developing and using be applied?

Radical changes in legislative policy do not, of course, always require magical or ingenious interventions with the group that is commissioned to make the policy. Litigation is *one* way. Policy may be tested in the courts in the hope that it may be invalidated on constitutional grounds or that its consequences will so dramatically move legislators as to inspire them to change it. (If a legislated social policy should be overturned by the courts on other than constitutional grounds, legislators may very well reinstate the policy with new legislation more scrupulously designed to avoid the court's interference.) For example, residence requirements based on prejudice against the free movement of welfare recipients and prejudice against unhampered welfare assistance have been successfully tested, and the likelihood is great that a new policy against them will characterize welfare programs across the United States.

As Jonathan Casper asserts:

> The notion of "going to court" as a means to gain desired policy goals—whether to end capital punishment, to liberalize abortion laws, to reform the welfare system, to change drug control laws, to protect natural resources—seems to me to occur to political partisans not only in a rapidly expanding number of issue areas, but in a sense to occur sooner.

We are witnessing not only a kind of institutionalization of the defense of civil liberties and rights of "traditional" minority groups like blacks and, more recently, the poor, but litigation is becoming an integral part of the strategies of the politically dissatisfied who are not so much institutionally oppressed—denied access to political arenas—but who simply have consistently lost in other arenas.[5]

By the same token, however, if the judges see in the Constitution "things not visible to the eyes of laymen, or even other lawyers, the only recourse of those aggrieved is to persuade the Court to overrule itself, which is difficult, or to amend the Constitution, which is still more difficult."[6] In addition, not all social policy is legislated and hence amenable to adjudication. Although law is often (by no means always) a reflection or expression of social policy, it is not the only or even the most important medium for reflecting or expressing it. Much of the social policy that guides the destinies of persons in need is not to be found in statutes.

Because social policy is inseparable from what has been described as centrally planned change for social welfare,[7] the features of American political life that James Wilson regards as making centrally planned change particularly unlikely apply as well to social policy:

One is . . . the decentralization of formal authority. Authority is decentralized to many levels of government, not just to three. There are at least nine hundred governmental units within the Chicago metropolitan area and more than fourteen hundred within the New York metropolitan region. Authority is decentralized to a whole range of governments, special districts, commissions, boards, and taxing authorities; within each of these, to executive, legislative, and judicial branches; and within each of these branches to particular agency heads, committee chairmen, and authoritative individual persons. This makes the obtaining of agreement by concerting wills extremely difficult, or, to put it in quasi-economic terms, costly in terms of the scarce authority resources at the command of any particular actor. There are many cases, of course, in which people willingly abdicate control over their small bit of authority to someone else. The school board may defer to the mayor because in some cases they may think the mayor ought to have the right to act as he sees fit with respect to certain issues. But the greater the dispersion of formal authority, the less the probability that people will willingly defer to other actors sufficient for there to be centrally planned change.

Not only does the decentralization of authority make the concerting of wills difficult, it also creates multiple opportunities for outside groups to register a veto or partial veto. When there are a great many officials, each of whom has a small piece or bit of authority, there are many who have a "price"—so to speak—that outside groups can afford to pay. . . . When I say price, I am not, of course, speaking of bribing prime ministers or kings or mayors. I am talking about "price" in terms of obtaining consent by any of a variety of means, including persuading these officials to adopt your system of beliefs. The greater the concentration of authority, the higher the price of the individual who has in his hand that concentration of authority. The greater the dispersal of authority, the lower the price and the greater the opportunity for groups and individuals to register vetoes.

The second reason for the absence of centrally planned change is the high-level popular and organizational involvement in American political and civic life. . . . In part, this high level of involvement exists because there are so many opportunities to wield influence; opportunities call into being people and organizations seeking to capitalize on those opportunities. Again, in quasi-economic terms, there is a competitive market in which one can use influence profitably. But, in addition, there is among Americans a felt obligation to participate—an obligation that can be explained only in terms of American intellectual and social history.

Third, there is coextensively with the decentralization of formal authority in the public sphere a decentralization of influence in the private sphere. In part this exists because of the great diversity of the country—ethnically, socially, regionally, economically, and religiously. In part it exists because the multiple opportunities for affecting policy create a corresponding number of groups seeking to affect it. There is more than one opportunity to register a veto and thus there is usually more than one group seeking to do so. . . . Because opportunities exist for sustaining local organizations by influencing local policy, there can be at the national level a wide variety of competing organizations speaking, presumably, for the same interests.[8]

It is difficult for an earnest social worker, attempting to wield an influence on social policy and social policymakers, to cope with the many influences on both, even when both are concentrating on the substantive issues involved, for the range of deviation from the social worker's value convictions can be very broad indeed. Existing policy and the participants with responsibility for considering and reconsidering it can be so alien to the social worker's policy goals that even a simple modification in policy may prove to be an awesome challenge. It is virtually an impossible challenge when the factors that influence the policymakers have no immediate bearing upon the substantive issues to be dealt with.

External variables

Indicative of the operation of external variables (external to the substantive policy issues to be contended with) is the distinction made by Wilson between *audience* and *constituency* in an effort to understand the behavior of many big-city mayors. Although he seems more interested in constituents as electors to whom mayors must appeal for votes, it is hardly reckless to regard them also as targets or beneficiaries of municipal policies. His distinction between *audience* and *constituency* then becomes even more pertinent for this discussion. As he puts it:

By "audience" I mean those persons whose favorable attitudes and responses the mayor is most interested in, those persons from whom he receives his most welcome applause and his most needed resources and opportunities. By "constituency" I mean those people who can vote for or against him in an election.[9]

This statement suggests what is hardly a mystery, namely, that social policy is not always what is regarded (however erroneously) as best for the people it affects but what, in the eyes of policymakers (if we may still call them that without tongue in cheek), is acceptable to persons or groups who, in the opinion of the policymakers, count in some way.

In addition to the internal pressures—socially, psychologically, and culturally derived—that affect the decisions of participants in policymaking circles, public and private, individual and collective, there are innumerable varieties of external pressures to be contended with, many of which relate only indirectly to the policy issues or to the people concerned. The problem for a social worker who feels or carries responsibility in this arena is not simply that the values that policymakers espouse, or by which they are influenced, do not happen to coincide with the social worker's value framework and hence may lead them to different ends and conclusions. The problem is that these values may not represent the policymakers' values at all. In other words, ideological preferences or convictions may not dictate the policymakers' specific choices of actions or decisions; they may be determined by entirely different factors less perceptible to the social worker's naked, albeit skilled, eye.

If a social worker can perceive a difference in personal value orientation that makes a policymaker a target or adversary, he can perhaps muster his data and his resources to effect a change in the policymaker's thinking. But if the policymaker's value choices stem from indeterminate sources, they may be so devious or obscure as to escape the social worker, or so numerous as to defy the social worker's professional intentions. He is then perforce hard put to know what data and what resources to apply—and where.

Categories of values

The personal and other-directed values that represent, on one hand, a focus of the social worker's policy-directed attention and, on the other, the locus of resistance to the social worker, may be classified under three categories: *authentic* values, *adaptive* values, and *aspirational* values.

Authentic values are what the participant in the policy-making process genuinely and personally prefers or believes for whatever reason in his background, rearing, or relationships. *Adaptive* values are what the participant chooses to believe or prefer in the interest of some immediate gratification or goal, such as finding favor in the eyes of his leader or his peers, or pleasing one audience or another. *Aspirational* values are what the participant opportunistically calculates merits his preference in the interest of a long-range ambition or objective related to his fate or his future, such as high office, community kudos, or lionization.

Any one of these three operant kinds of values, when it serves to explain the stance of a policymaker from which the social worker wishes to shake him loose, is apt to be very complex. When all three are operating—and they often do in the social policy arena—the prognosis for change must be unenthusiastic.

An examination of President Nixon's "welfare speech" of August 8, 1969, is instructive in this connection and can serve as an illustrative conclusion for this discussion. In many respects, that speech is a model policy statement, although its content is not altogether exemplary from the point of view of social work values. Nevertheless, it is a good example of what a policy statement is and does or ought to do. It sets forth, in effect, a value framework upon the basis of which program proposals may be made, adopted, and implemented. This policy is set forth in the "package of four measures" enunciated in the speech. The first measure calls for "a complete replacement of the present welfare system" by a new family assistance system that "rests essentially on three principles: equality of treatment, a work requirement and a work incentive." The second measure calls for "a comprehensive new job training and placement program," in order to realize "our full opportunity concept." The third measure calls for a "revamping of the Office of Economic Opportunity," which is cast in the speech "in terms of its symbolic importance":

> For the first time, applying the principles of the New Federalism, administration of a major established Federal program would be turned over to the states and local governments, recognizing that they are in a position to do the job better.
> For years, thoughtful Americans have talked of the need to decentralize government. The time has come to begin.[10]

Finally, the fourth measure calls for a start on the sharing of the federal tax revenue with the states, "which I consider profoundly important to the future of our federal system of shared responsibilities"—shared, that is, between states and localities on one hand and national government on the other.

It would not be fair to speculate too freely about President Nixon's value orientation and its sources, and not merely for the reason that others drafted his speech. On the other hand, his political record and experience are not so private that some assumptions cannot be made about the varieties of values that drive him toward his policy preferences and about the sources from which they stem. His values and their sources both reflect, in general, the types of forces with which any social worker must cope in dealing with any policymaker at any level. In this package of four measures is reflected a multiplicity of cultural, historical, and personal influences that invariably have their impact on policymakers at various levels of public and private decision-making, influences that must temper the expectations of social workers who strive to affect social policy. Reflected in these measures are such historical antecedents as the principle of lesser eligibility, the Protestant ethic, the states' rights movement, and numerous other influences. Nor can one forget that President Nixon's past campaigns suggested such value inclinations as may be characterized as conservative tendencies. It is not so rash, therefore, to conceive of this policy statement, also, among other things, as a nod in the direction of liberal or radical voters who by their votes expressed their reservations about his values and about the social policies they were likely to engender. The speech thus provides for the rights of the poor and welfare recipients as well as for the rights of those who would like to limit the rights of the poor and welfare recipients.

How does a social worker influence such policy choices, in such a situation?

It is not easy, but it is necessary to try, especially when one aims to mobilize the capacity of affected groups to have their own impact on their own destiny. Pessimistic as this review may sound, it is not designed to obviate or discourage efforts at influence on the shape of social policy but rather to awaken sensibility to the great and ingenious effort that may be required.

Notes

1. Social policy generally connotes specific values, for it implies ends that for some reason are preferred and toward which there is a clear determination to work. Social policy is regarded as something worth working for and working toward. It provides a rationale for doing the work. "In so far as decisions lead toward the selection of final goals, they will be called 'value judgments'; so far as they involve the implementation of such goals they will be called 'factual judgments' " ". . . if administration consists in 'getting things done' by groups of people, purpose provides a principal criterion in determining what things are to be done" (Herbert A. Simon, *Administrative Behavior,* 2nd ed. [New York: The Free Press, 1965], pp. 4–5).

2. Eveline M. Burns, Social Policy: The Stepchild of the Curriculum, *Proceedings of Ninth Annual Program Meeting, Council on Social Work Education* (New York: Council on Social Work Education, 1961), pp. 23–34.

3. William Gorham, PPBS: Its Scope and Limits (1)—Notes of a Practitioner, *The Public Interest,* no. 8 (Summer 1967), p. 5.

4. Peter F. Drucker, The Sickness of Government, *The Public Interest,* no. 14 (Winter 1969), p. 9.

5. *New York Times*, September 7, 1969, p. 76.

6. Joseph W. Bishop, Jr., The Warren Court Is Not Likely To Be Overruled, *New York Times Magazine*, September 7, 1969, p. 31.

7. Cf. Robert Morris, ed., *Centrally Planned Change: Prospects and Concepts* (New York: National Association of Social Workers, 1964), Introduction. "Policies are standing plans. Policies are general guides to future decision-making that are intended to shape those decisions so as to maximize their contribution to the goals of the enterprise. Policies are the instruments by which goals are achieved. They are broad in nature . . . they are indeed predetermined courses of action" (Preston P. Le Breton and Dale A. Henning, *Planned Theory* [Englewood Cliffs, N.J.: Prentice-Hall, 1961], p. 9).

8. James Q. Wilson, An Overview of Theories of Planned Change, in Morris, *Centrally Planned Change*, pp. 18–20. "The social policy formulation process is becoming increasingly complicated involving communities in the search for solutions to current problems and planning for change is a necessity that has become both compelling and impossibly complex in our time. Problems of urban life have exploded into proportions that seem beyond the abilities of citizens—lay and professional alike—to grasp" (Ralph M. Kramer and Harry Specht, eds., *Readings in Community Organization Practice* [Englewood Cliffs, N.J.: Prentice-Hall, 1969], p. 7).

9. James Q. Wilson, The Mayor's Dilemmas: II—The Mayors vs. the Cities, *The Public Interest*, no. 16 (Summer 1969), p. 28.

10. *New York Times*, August 9, 1969.

FAMILY ADVOCACY: FROM CASE TO CAUSE

Robert Sunley

The gap between the individual case of social injustice and broad-scale social action has been a continual source of frustration for the family worker and the family agency alike. The family worker struggles time after time to rectify wrongs suffered by clients. Sometimes he succeeds, often through some personal contact with a counterpart in the offending social institution, but he is only too aware of and further frustrated by the fact that ten or a hundred other people continue to suffer for lack of such influential intervention. His work on behalf of one client will bring about no change in the institution. The sheer immovability and unresponsiveness of the bureaucracy to his individual effort will tend to dull his enthusiasm and dedication as it does with many workers, who drift toward "adjustment" rather than attempt to change the organizations. The client may also be directly or subtly encouraged to come to terms with

Reprinted from *Social Casework,* June 1970.

"reality"—the reality of formidable arrays of laws, rules, regulations, and practices.

For the agency, the gap has also posed a difficult problem. Though aware of the need for social action, most agencies—the board and administration—have had no agency-wide structure within which to operate. Isolated efforts by the board, such as passing resolutions or writing letters to legislators, hardly meet the need. There is little or no linkage between client, staff, board, and the needed action. At best, staff and board are linked by the traditional role of the caseworker in social action, as set out by Mary Richmond, Charlotte Towle, Gordon Hamilton, and most recently by Harry Specht, which may be summed up in Towle's brief description:

> . . . the caseworker [would] be responsible for initiating or instigating social action by making known unmet needs and social ills as revealed in his practice. He would contribute his findings, through agency channels, to those writing social policy, conducting publicity campaigns, drafting legislation. . . .[1]

According to this point of view the family agency also has a limited function. Worker and agency together are only too likely to see themselves as small and rather inactive members of a large-scale process, limited to polite and long-range efforts at legislation, examples perhaps of that sense of powerlessness and of that disjunction between goals and structure fitting under the general catchword *anomie*.[2]

Quite a few family agencies have recently made efforts to bridge this gap. Perhaps most notable was Project ENABLE, a national program which brought agencies into direct touch with the poor, those suffering daily from social injustices. This project, like other special programs, was not integral to the regular agency function; separately funded through the Office of Economic Opportunity, the programs for the most part ended with the termination of the special funding.[3] The regular agency programs remained as before, though the awareness of the need for something comparable was undoubtedly heightened. The prospect of large-scale ongoing funding for projects such as ENABLE appear quite dim for the near future; whatever agencies do must be done within the fairly narrow margins of regular budget allocations.

Family advocacy is a move toward bridging the gap, but within the regular agency functioning. It delineates a basic function of the caseworker and assures a continuing link with the action program. It recognizes the professional obligation (not option) of the worker for social action, for fighting through to the finish for clients' rights and needs.[4] The concept of family advocacy also embraces the vital principle of involving the client in the action, of helping the client to help himself in this area as well as in that of individual and family functioning.

As will be seen, family advocacy requires more than good intentions; in effect, it is a discipline in itself, as yet only partially developed. A body of knowledge, principles, and methods exists in part. Even interviewing, the specialty of the family worker, must take on an additional focus and objective. A new commitment by the agency is necessary to back up the family worker. It must be expressed in new structuring as well as in new distribution of staff time and emphasis.

Several of the important aspects of a family advocacy program—interviewing, case study, interventions and objectives, and agency structuring—are discussed here. Examples are given from one agency, the Family Service Association of Nassau County, which recently established a department of family advocacy, headed by a full-time social worker, which embraces the work of the family workers, administration, and board.

Interviewing for family advocacy

By training and practice many family caseworkers focus on individual and family dysfunction or pathology. The material elicited from the client tends to bear upon this focus. Thus, when a child is referred as a slow learner, not achieving his potential, a family caseworker may accept the basic premise of the referral which is usually buttressed by evidence from the school. This evidence might include poor grades, I.Q. and other psychological tests, or examples of poor behavior. The caseworker does not usually make as careful a study of the school, the educational approach and philosophy, and the teacher as he does of the child and parents in his effort to determine the cause of the learning or behavior problem evidenced by the child.

Interviewing for advocacy introduces a range of new factors into the sessions with the client and "collateral" sources. Some of these perhaps sound obvious, but all reach much further than appears at first sight. Clients may not, for various reasons, give complete information, and the caseworker's skill is needed to develop a relationship of trust and confidence. In contacting public and private organizations on behalf of clients, workers have frequently been baffled in trying to find out precisely the relevant regulations, practices, requirements, or entitlements. The difficulties may result from bureaucratic timidity or, as Charles Grosser points out, result from the fact that some institutions are "overtly negative and hostile, often concealing or distorting information. . . ." [5] Reconciling conflicting stories of clients and professional colleagues in other organizations can be as difficult as reconciling those of husbands and wives in marital conflict.

Caseworkers themselves are often lax in facing or establishing facts, although their sympathies and actions may be in the right direction. For example, Daniel Thursz cites the example of a group of social workers who were called upon to document with cases the "man-in-the-house" rule; they "did not have one bit of supporting evidence." [6] Or, more serious yet, David Wineman and Adrienne James charged in a recent article that students are "systematically taught to abandon reality," describing the many abuses they encounter and the many "cop-outs" used by supervisors and administrators (and eventually by the students and caseworkers as well). [7]

Difficulties facing the worker

In addition to the problems centered around obtaining accurate information, the caseworker may well encounter his own difficulties stemming more directly from the "medical" model of pathology. For example, the assessment of pathology in a client may well affect the worker's perception and evaluation of an injustice the client is undergoing. Paranoid tendencies in the client may lead a worker to discount reality problems. The worker may see a sullen welfare recipient only as withdrawn, depressed, and distorting reality—the pathological view—instead of as a person who is suspicious out of experience and seeks to protect himself against further attack.

Also, value judgments enter in. For example, the client's mismanagement of money or time or role may offend the caseworker. In one situation, caseworkers from several agencies were in accord that a certain client was an unfit mother, leaving young children unattended on many occasions; yet her lawyer entered a suit against the department of welfare alleging that it had failed to make provision for sitters while she did necessary shopping and errands. Regardless of the merits of this situation, it is notable that caseworkers had not taken any advocacy position for their client, nor since then for clients in comparable difficulties. Perhaps as a result of interagency snafus and frustrating experiences in dealing with governmental bureaucracies, many caseworkers have tended to fall back onto the "adjustment" solution to environmental problems: The client adjusts, that is, if he or she possesses the "ego strengths" to do so. In fairness, the individual workers may well be aware of better solutions and approaches, but they have had within their job no channels or groups through which to exert pressure.

The caseworker may also be subject to other internal stresses. The nature of the issues involved may subtly turn him off; the fact that the client does not come into the situation with "clean hands" may keep him from seeing that legal or human rights have been violated; his own fear of authority may also induce him to hold back; or his identification with authority may predispose him to side with the world of rules and established practices, perhaps rationalized as a conviction that the authorities may make mistakes, but that they mean well. Yet another extreme may be that of the caseworker whose own rebellious feelings cause him to secretly provoke a client into arbitrary rebellion.

All these examples may be termed *countertransference* in a general way. Workers may have mastered such reactions in relation to individual and family relationship problems but be less able to recognize them in advocacy situations. The result may emerge not only in misjudgments or failure to elicit information, but more importantly in an inability to develop that outlook and commitment necessary for advocacy for the client.

A situation reported recently illustrates the possibilities and pitfalls. Three children in a family receiving public assistance were sent home the first day of school because of inadequate clothing. A recent New York state law eliminated all special grants, including clothing, for such families. In responding to the situation, the caseworker could see to it that the family received a donation of the necessary clothing, could help the mother with budgeting, or could try to help the mother with a presumed depression that kept her from managing her funds—possible solutions, but not advocacy. Or, the caseworker could ask such questions as: Are these and other children being denied their right to an education by the new welfare law? Is a mother being forced to put herself in risk of a charge of child neglect because of the new state law? The caseworker now has made the large first step in advocacy—a commitment to the client rather than to the existing system involved. The caseworker should then have recourse to a lawyer to determine whether there is a basis for a court case to test the constitutionality of the new law, or to a welfare rights group to determine if a public issue should be made of the situation. These alternatives, it should be noted, will involve the client acting on her own behalf.

Where does family counseling enter in? Its place is clear with clients who come for family problems and subsequently reveal social problems calling for advocacy, although the worker must as with any client be alert to the possibility that the actual injustice may also become a focal point in the client's defensive system to resist any internal change. On the other hand, clients who come essentially for redress of wrongs cannot be treated as if they are indirectly asking for personal counseling. Although this assumption has been made by many workers in the past, it may well run counter to the reality seen by the client. Low-income families (and others as well) tend to view such interviewing activity by the worker as prying into their personal lives, and from that may make a reasonable deduction that there is something behind the scenes they do not understand and do not trust. Also, the worker's eagerness to get to the family problems (as if this were the only justification for his job) may seriously disrupt the client's sense of priorities in his personal life, leaving the client overwhelmed and the worker helpless by premature exposure of all problems.

Case study

Just as casework treatment is based on a study of background material, current situation, and related factors, a case for advocacy should rest upon a comparable study. More specifically, in advocacy the worker needs to familiarize himself not only with the specific client, problem, and situation but also with such factors as the institutions involved and the legal implications.

Broadly speaking, situations are presented to the caseworker either directly as situations for advocacy—the client comes seeking help for a problem in which rights are apparently being violated—or the client comes for some other difficulty but the caseworker elicits the advocacy need. As a first step, as already noted, the caseworker must be alert and committed to the client's position in relation to social institutions. Perhaps a good working method is to see every problem the client has as a possible problem that the social institution has; this is not to negate the client's possible internal problem but to ensure that we carefully examine in what ways this is a shared problem and whether solutions may not lie outside the client, either partly or wholly.

Many grievances relate to possible legal rights of the client. The caseworker has a responsibility to uncover such possibilities, to obtain necessary facts, and to consult a lawyer or legal service for the poor to ascertain whether a legal case exists. The caseworker is also responsible for helping the client understand that there may be possible publicity, delays, and other strains involved in pursuing a court case. He must inform him of possible alternative solutions. He must determine whether the client is assured of financial support and other needs during the trial period, if this enters into the situation. And he must help the client reach a decision, which may mean going into motivations, conflicts, and fears. Looking further ahead, the caseworker must plan to be available throughout and even after a case is settled, for it can happen that a client may win a court case but meet further delays and appeals. Thus, in the area of legal rights, caseworkers need not only some knowledge of law in those areas often involved in client problems, but also a working relationship with a legal service or lawyer who handles advocacy cases, to understand the practical workings of the legal system and to be able to obtain opinions quickly and informally.

For various reasons, however, legal recourse may not be sought even though rights have been violated. This may be the choice of the client or test cases may already be pending; nevertheless, other immediate action may be desired. In addition, in cases where legal rights have not been violated but other human rights are involved, resulting from institutional insensitivity to the needs of the poor and elderly, there may also be cause for further action. Interventions suitable in such cases will be described later.

Familiarity with pertinent law is but one of a number of areas of knowledge the caseworker needs. Credit practices, school policies and practices, family court, handling of alcoholics and drug addicts, probationary methods, psychiatric facilities, and systems theories are others. In short, the caseworker as advocate needs to develop knowledge and understanding of the institutions and systems with which clients are most often in contact. This refers not only to general knowledge but also to specific institutions in the community. While caseworkers perforce develop a working knowledge of local institutions, this is usually developed piecemeal and not fully shared and pooled with other staff to develop a full picture. The caseworker—not in isolation but with other staff—needs in effect an outline with which to study a given organization, just as he explicitly or implicitly follows such an outline in developing his study of an individual or family, however imperfect such an outline may be in its ultimate explanations.

An institution or organization is first characterized by the fact that it has an entity (usually a legal base for its existence), its own structure, regulations, premises, staff; it is set off from other organizations by its clientele—it serves certain people for certain specified purposes only. There is a hierarchy of command and accountability. The worker should become familiar with these aspects of each important organization in the community. Beyond the formal structure, however, and perhaps more important, is the informal structure of the organization and its relationship to the community. The caseworker needs to ask the following questions: What is the orientation of the organization toward the people it serves? What is its tone or morale? How does one evaluate the discrepancy between clients' complaints and agency position? What efforts have been made to change policies, by whom and how, and with what results? What is the response of the organization to criticism or attack? Does it have vulnerabilities (adverse publicity, for example)? At what level, within or above the organization, is there discretionary power to make changes?

On a practical level the caseworker needs to know the following: procedural structure in relation to clients, to whom grievances are first addressed and what further steps are specified, such as appeals or review boards; in what ways retaliation against the client may be resorted to, and what protection can be found for the client; and whether or not other clients of the agency encounter the same difficulty. He will also want to know if clients of other agencies have encountered similar difficulties and what if anything they have tried.

It becomes clear that an institution must be viewed more as an adversary in advocacy, rather than as a cooperating or allied agency (even though in other situations this may be true). *Adversary* does not perforce mean *enemy,* but does require a different approach from the consensus approach to which caseworkers are accustomed.[8] Even from this brief description, it can be seen that the full ongoing assessment of an advocacy case may require case conferences or outside consultation—or both—just as in an evaluation of a family treatment case.

Interventions

In casework, the worker (and other staff at times) selects the methods and modes of treatment for each client, based on the initial case evaluation. In family advocacy, similar steps seem necessary, from the initial interviews, through the study and diagnostic thinking, to the selection of interventions; the necessary participation of the client or client group is, obviously, on a different level in this process.

Family agencies have traditionally used only a small number of the many kinds of interventions available for an advocacy program. The selection of which interventions to use in a given issue is a complex one, involving the nature of the problem, the objective, the nature of the adversary, the degree of militancy to which the agency will go, and the effectiveness of the method, generally and in relation to certain kinds of situations. All of these factors suggest the desirability of expert consultation for many agencies in an ongoing advocacy program. More than one method is usually included in an action program, with the result that the staff and the agency as a whole will become involved in various ways.

In advocacy programs it is important for the agency not to get caught in dilatory tactics so common in bureaucratic procedures; an overconcern for the niceties and politeness of "due process" may dishearten staff and cause suffering for the clients. Yet failure to study the situation carefully may result in a quick action being dismissed because a necessary step was omitted. For example, a case brought against a school system was dismissed after a period of months because the court ruled that the plaintiff had failed to exhaust other remedies first, namely, an appeal to the board of education. By this time, the school year was almost over, the complaint no longer had any validity, and the child had been subjected to adverse conditions.

The following methods of intervention hardly exhaust the possibilities or the many variations used by groups (mainly nonsocial work) but suggest the wide range and the many types suitable for a family advocacy program.

1. Studies and surveys. These often form the groundwork for further action, both for the advocacy program itself and for educational and publicity purposes. Whatever the sources of the material, staff and board must be prepared to answer penetrating or hostile questions, and material should in effect be subjected to such an approach before it is used. Otherwise embarrassing loopholes may be exposed and the effort weakened.

2. Expert testimony. Social workers may be called upon to testify as professionals or agency representatives, with or without the backing of studies and surveys. While this method may not have great effect upon legislators or public officials, the absence of the social work voice may be noted adversely.

3. Case conferences with other agencies. This has traditionally been one important way in which the agency tries to effect change; by presenting the conditions and results of certain practices and regulations in given cases, one hopes to induce the other agency to change. This method may be of value in early stages of an advocacy effort, especially if it can involve higher officials of the other agency. It also elicits much about the potential adversary organization and may help to clarify just where the crux of the problem lies—at the level of staff practice, supervision, middle or top administration, board, or beyond the agency. Such conferences held with clients present can have other values as well and may be the first step in developing a client group determined to go further in action on its own behalf.

4. Interagency committees. Such committees, which often have proven to be splendid time-wasters, can offer the advantages of case conferences mentioned above. They can also be developed into types of permanent bodies which can represent yet another method of action in a given locality. In large suburban areas, encompassing several small communities, various agencies may provide services within each small community but obviously cannot have a local base in each. An interagency committee can be developed involving local community agencies and the wider-based agencies to handle local issues. For example, Family Service Association of Nassau County along with another agency started such a committee in one community, originally around overlapping case concerns. Over a five-year period, the committee has developed into a kind of local welfare council, though without separate corporate existence. It takes up local issues and is called upon by other organizations to help in certain situations. This type of committee, for example, can be used by a local agency which may have complaints against the school system but hesitates to take action alone. It also provides a vehicle for the interagency sharing of grass-roots problems arising from specific cases, which councils embracing large areas and many agencies cannot do.

5. Educational methods. This refers to activities such as

informational meetings, panels, exhibits, pamphlets, and press coverage, all aimed at educating segments of the population. These may include also public appeals on specific issues made through the press, radio, and television. Legislators and public officials may be somewhat influenced by these methods.

6. Position-taking. The agency formally takes a position on an issue, making it known publicly through the press, as well as to officials, legislators, and others directly. This goes beyond an educational effort in an attempt to put the weight of the agency onto a specific position. Generally, the agency's position will be newsworthy only if it is among the first to take the stand, or if board members represent an influence with important segments of the community. The taking of a formal position may be often of greatest value internally, that is, in conveying to staff and clientele that the agency is committed and moving.

7. Administrative redress. Governmental bodies usually provide for various steps to appeal decisions at the practice level. While such steps may appear to delay action, they may nonetheless be necessary preludes to further action (such as court suits) or desirable in that they will call the attention of higher officials within or without the agency to conditions. Also, where the imperfect working of a system has resulted in an injustice to one client, grievance procedures through an ombudsman often result in a correction for that one client. Taking such moves may be necessary although the advocacy program need not stop there in fighting a larger battle.

8. Demonstration projects. Even though focused directly on problems of the poor, demonstration projects are generally long-term methods of advocacy. They may be necessary in order to elicit the specific material needed for advocacy, and to help a group or community develop the awareness, leadership, and determination to embark upon a course of action. Further advocacy is usually needed to carry the message of the demonstration project into a larger scale service or institutional change affecting the total population involved in a problem.

9. Direct contacts with officials and legislators. The agency may approach them formally to make positions known, give relevant information, or protest actions carried out or contemplated. Informal meetings, individually or with groups of legislators, may be similarly used and may enable the legislator to reveal ignorance, ask questions, and listen to more specific material. The agency might attempt to set up some type of regular contact, which in time may result in greater impact as agency personnel and views become known.

10. Coalition groups. These can be described as ad hoc groupings of organizations around a specific objective. The advantages lie not only in the combination of forces, but in the fact that agencies do not have to bear the burden and risk separately. The coalition concept also points to the involvement of disparate types of organizations and groups, which maintain autonomy while pursuing a common goal. Each organization usually has a circle of adherents who in turn may be more willing to work in concert than alone. Drawbacks involve the danger of setting too general goals and methods, and a proliferation of meetings and committees seeking to "clarify" and "cooperate."

11. Client groups. The wide-scale development of the potential of client groups has occurred only recently, and has revealed that this is a major instrument of social change. By *client groups* is meant any local groups or groupings of individuals sharing a problem; while they are not the traditional agency clients, they are so termed in the sense that they are in some way helped through an agency service. This service may be limited to giving some impetus to the forming of the group, but may continue in the form of consultation to the group, supportive efforts in such ways as helping the group obtain information or gain access to certain people, or mounting collaborative efforts with other community groups. At the outset the advocate may assist in helping the group role-play contemplated action, help solve problems with the group, or suggest ways of augmenting the group. Through community contacts the advocate may help in bringing several groups together to develop

coalitions; he may also suggest various methods of action for the group's consideration. Some family agencies have already had valuable experience with such groups in Project ENABLE, which by its very name indicates the primary role of the advocate in relation to such groups.

There is already considerable literature on client groups that covers many aspects of this method of social change. There are, however, two dangers to which the caseworker-advocate should be alert from the start: first, being too verbal, directive, not remaining where the group is, or directly or indirectly using the group as a means to ends other than what the group develops; second, the failure to develop other sources of support toward the same general objectives and to help the group relate to other support in a meaningful but autonomous manner.

12. Petitions. While petitions appear to have little direct effect upon officials and legislators, they are valuable in calling attention to an issue. Getting petitions signed is also a valuable activity for a new group in that it mobilizes members around an action and gives them an opportunity to talk to people about the issue, develop their abilities in making public contacts, and formulate points and rebuttals. It may also provide a way of reaching other interested people who might join or support the group.

13. Persistent demands. This method in effect means bombardment of officials and legislators, going beyond the usual channels of appeal. Thus a welfare group protesting welfare cuts directed one effort against the local board of education, in an attempt to get the board to join in action to influence the state legislature. This method represents a kind of escalation of a campaign, and may be directed against figures inaccessible or unwilling to submit to personal contacts. While within lawful limits, it may be the precursor to harassment or other extralegal means.

14. Demonstrations and protests. These include marches, street dramas, vigils, picketing, sit-ins, and other public demonstrations. The family advocate should become familiar with these methods, although organizing and con-

ducting them may lie beyond his competence and role. To what extent an agency as such will organize and participate in these methods will have to be determined within the agency. An agency will have to consider carefully, however, whether its other forms of action are not being conducted from too far behind the firing line, and whether commitment may not require some such firing line activity at times.

Selecting the method of intervention

The objectives of any plan of intervention are closely tied in with the methods selected and the nature of the issue and of the adversary organizations. An effort to challenge a state law usually will require a massive effort, on many levels and with various methods, whereas challenging a practice of a local organization may be accomplished through such means as meetings, pressures, client groups, and administrative redress. A demonstration project may represent a fresh and optimistic approach to a problem that has eluded solution for years; it cuts through a problem in a different way and represents a long-term investment toward an objective. For example, the very early childhood experimental programs now in progress in several places in the country, such as one being conducted by Family Service Association of Nassau County, represent a new approach to one goal of reformers and advocates—that of forcing the school systems to provide vast remedial and enrichment programs for the many low-income children who suffer cognitive deficiencies. The objective of these new programs is to foster early development in the child so that the need for later remedial efforts is minimized or even eliminated. The program conducted by Family Service Association of Nassau County has the additional objective of enhancing the role of mothers and fathers in low-income families, an objective pursued in the past through various other methods.

The family advocate and the agency must consider the

order of priority of their objectives, leaving room for sharpening or shifting of focus as practice reveals more clearly the nature of the issues involved and points to new approaches, such as those mentioned in relation to demonstration projects. The family advocate should also be alert to the many seemingly minor petty harassments, indignities, and omissions he will suffer—these are often the only part of the Establishment iceberg that is visible to the poor. Ultimately they may become larger issues than the clear-cut injustices which are amenable to lawsuits or other definable actions. Behind the small indignities lie the encrusted attitudes and structures which are far more impervious to change than a given rule or regulation. As William Blake wrote in 1804, "He who would do good to another, must do it in Minute Particulars/General Good is the plea of the scoundrel hypocrite & flatterer." [9]

Agency structure

The commitment of the agency to action on behalf of families is obviously the cornerstone of an advocacy program. But commitment can rather quickly be dissipated unless a workable structure for advocacy is established. The structure must be one which can and does involve the entire agency, including staff, board, and volunteers in an ongoing activity. Commitment must also be represented by a commitment of time; if advocacy is to be the second major function of a family agency, it must receive the time, attention, and thought that have gone into the counseling program. For example, does the staff time committed to advocacy equal that committed to recording interviews? The staff can tell by such allotments what the agency really means to emphasize. The board, with overall responsibility for the agency, will probably need to delegate to a committee the charge for advocacy. Such a committee, already existing in a number of agencies as public issues or social concerns committees, should probably be separate from a committee focused on legislation per se, as the latter would be dealing primarily with bills introduced into legislative bodies. At times, of course, the two committees may be concerned with the same issue and even the same legislation.

The advocacy committee has several important functions. One is to become and keep informed on local problems and issues in order to make continuous assessments of priorities for action and give guidelines to staff involved in advocacy; staff in turn will inform the committee of the pressing concerns of the people. Also essential to advocacy is the potential for quick action. The committee consequently must establish methods by which the advocacy staff can move quickly and still be assured of its backing. This can be done only through an ongoing process in which the committee learns to set guidelines by considering the methods, successes, and failures of the staff and others involved in advocacy. A close and continuing contact between staff and committee is necessary.

The committee has a key responsibility in thinking through the implications of any course of action giving particular thought to follow-through so that client groups are not stirred up and then disappointed by an action that is abandoned. It must also consider the risks involved for the agency in taking action and in making alignments with various groups. Finally, the committee itself becomes involved in action. Members may attend public meetings and hearings or call upon officials and legislators. For example, the public issues committee of the Family Service Association of Nassau County took up the transportation problem in the county as it affects the poor. The committee met with the county planning commission and with a representative of the bus companies, obtained much background material, and then, with staff, attended public hearings to present the agency position. Usually board members carry more weight in efforts to influence officials and legislators than do social workers; they may speak not only as residents of a community but may also be able to mobilize other local groups unaffiliated with the agency.

Agency staff also needs to be involved, so that advocacy

is not an isolated, specialized function. While historically the caseworker has been seen as one who relays case material to administrators and board, it is evident that staff is for the most part not content with this role, which has no follow-through and which may only occasionally involve any given worker. On the other hand, not all caseworkers can be closely involved in every advocacy action, and there are aspects to advocacy which call for the development of expertise and knowledge to be exercised more centrally in an agency.

Different patterns for staff advocacy are possible, depending on agency size, funding, staff interests, and other considerations. The following are four examples:

1. An agency may have a full-time staff position of family advocate, or a department of advocacy headed by the family advocate. This position, as recently established at Family Service Association of Nassau County through a foundation grant, is initially projected to include two main functions: first, to work with staff, providing consultation on action on behalf of individual clients, or handling certain situations directly and compiling case material on problems for the public issues committee. In addition, the family advocate will be working to involve the staff in further action, such as the formation of client groups concerned with specific problems, and participation in committees and hearings. It should be noted that clerical staff may also be involved in such actions; most clerical staff in social agencies have or develop a commitment to the purposes of social work, and should have opportunity to ally themselves in their capacity as agency personnel as well as private citizens.

The second major responsibility of the family advocate is to act as the staff person to the public issues committee. He helps the members define priority problems through case material and background information and by bringing in officials and others who are involved in the problems; he works with them to set guidelines and steps for action, to think through implications, to review what has been done, and to evaluate methods. The family advocate may act as agency spokesman, and as liaison to officials and legislators; he may act as agency representative with coalition groups and community groups, and as consultant to client groups; or he may act as advisor to staff or board people who carry out these functions.

One example will illustrate how guidelines and priorities are established, and how the family advocate can take action accordingly. The public issues committee defined several priority problem areas before adjourning for the summer; one involved what appeared to be the inequitable distribution and possible poor use of federal education funds siphoned through the state (Title I funds of the Elementary and Secondary Education Act provide added services for children of low-income families). The committee had no specific cases with which to document this possible problem; it had been suggested by agency staff whose contacts with schools on behalf of clients gave them good reason to believe this was an area to explore further and possibly act upon. Shortly afterwards, the family advocate spoke with the superintendent of a school district which was rapidly becoming a ghetto and needed massive governmental funding to cope with educational needs. The superintendent, failing to obtain funds anywhere, was ready to explore this area.

The family advocate, acting as consultant and organizer, helped prepare factual material which documented the inequitable distribution of funds and helped assemble a group of other superintendents in similar situations. State education officials came to meetings, and one school district instituted a court suit to force redistribution. Throughout, the advocate worked cooperatively with the Title I Director of the County Economic Opportunity Council. All this activity took place in line with the priorities set down by the public issues committee, which had not anticipated that this particular problem would suddenly come alive—this rested upon the work of the advocate and the decision of the executive director.

2. Variation on the establishment of a full-time family advocate might include creating a part-time position instead. Or, an "indigenous" worker might fill the position. This pattern might require the investment of more staff and consultation time but bring about other advantages such as better contact with local poverty groups.

3. A present staff member might be assigned in agencies where the budget does not permit expansion of staff at present. Or, a part-time assignment could be made, as an expedient only, since the conflict between the demands of a caseload and of the advocacy function would be frequent and onerous for the worker.

4. A staff committee might be formed, with a chairman bearing responsibility for the advocacy function, but delegating pieces of work to committee members. This method has the advantages of involving more staff directly, keeping the advocacy function related to the casework, and keeping the staff in direct contact with the board committee. Obviously it could present difficulties in carrying out actions, as well as in the kinds of demands upon the worker's attention and time mentioned above.

It may be possible in the context of the four patterns that have been described for the agency to obtain graduate social work students for the program. This would provide needed manpower. Students can, for example, do much of the background work which is time-consuming for the caseworker but essential to the advocacy function. Some schools of social work, in preparing "generic" workers, may find this a highly desirable type of placement, since it can provide the student with selected cases related to advocacy, client groups with which to work, again in connection with advocacy, and community organization and action experience.

In agencies where a separate position of family advocate cannot be established, staff members carrying the functions in one of the patterns suggested should have direct access to the responsible board committee and work with that committee. Otherwise the resulting delays in cross-communication and lack of clarity may impede any action. An agency may find it needs the advice of one or more specialists in the areas of agency structuring and functioning for advocacy, orientation to clientele, assisting client groups, and defining areas of action and strategies.

Conclusion

Family advocacy offers a way for agencies and staffs to bridge the gap between the many cases of individual grievances against social institutions and the broader-scale actions needed to bring about institutional change. The caseworker's intimate knowledge of individual families provides a grass-roots basis for social action, and his concern for families becomes an integral and vital part of the advocacy process.

The defining of the function of family advocacy points to the need for special knowledge and skills, to support the caseworker's activity and to promote social change. A meaningful commitment by the agency is essential to carrying out the second major function of the family agency—improving the social environment of families.

Notes

1. Charlotte Towle, Social Work: Cause and Function, *Social Casework*, 42:394 (October 1961); see also Harry Specht, Casework Practice and Social Policy Formulation, *Social Work*, 13:42–52 (January 1968); and Gordon Hamilton, The Role of Social Casework in Social Policy, *Social Casework*, 33:315–24 (October 1952).

2. Ann Hartman, Anomie and Social Casework, *Social Casework*, 50:131–37 (March 1969).

3. Ellen P. Manser, *Project ENABLE: What Happened* (New York: Family Service Association of America, 1968).

4. NASW Ad Hoc Committee on Advocacy, The Social Worker as Advocate: Champion of Social Victims, *Social Work*, 14:16–22 (April 1969).

5. Charles F. Grosser, Community Development Programs Serving the Urban Poor, *Social Work,* 10:18 (July 1965).

6. Daniel Thursz, Social Action As a Professional Responsibility, *Social Work,* 11:17 (July 1966).

7. David Wineman and Adrienne James, The Advocacy Challenge to Schools of Social Work, *Social Work,* 14:26 (April 1969).

8. Irwin Epstein, Social Workers and Social Action: Attitudes Toward Social Action Strategies, *Social Work,* 13:101–8 (April 1968).

9. *Jerusalem,* chap. 3, lines 60–61.

DIALOGUE ON RACISM, A PROLOGUE TO ACTION?

Pauline D. Lide

In the *Social Casework* editorial of March 1964, the following observation was made:

> The relative dearth of literature on the racial factor in casework treatment . . . and the conspicuous absence of research on the subject suggest that repressive psychological mechanisms may be at work. Perhaps it is difficult for a profession committed to humanistic tenets to engage in honest appraisal of possible disparities between its ideals and its accomplishments.[1]

This article recounts the efforts of one social agency to examine and loosen these "repressive psychological mechanisms" by means of an honest appraisal that took the form of staff dialogue for a period of approximately five months.[2] The dialogue followed an abortive effort to study the mechanisms as they appeared to operate in casework practice. A

Reprinted from *Social Casework*, July 1971.

description of the content and process of this experience may be useful for social workers who are willing to face the implications of the now clearly observable disparities between social work's ideals and its accomplishments.

Facing the fact and the implications of racism is a herculean task that can threaten the ego immeasurably.[3] Social workers—experienced caseworkers in particular—are generally knowledgeable about the process of loosening repressive psychological mechanisms that are developed to protect the ego. In their struggle for self-awareness they work assiduously to loosen the mechanisms that limit them in many areas of functioning. They have been slow, however, to face the fact of racism and the painful process of dealing with its implications. The recent appearance of several significant articles devoted to various aspects of individual and institutional racism suggests that the social work profession is beginning to become involved in this process.[4]

A practice research approach to racism

Late in 1967, the writer and a small group of administrative and supervisory staff of the Family Counseling Center of Metropolitan Atlanta began to examine possible ways to improve casework service for black clients.[5] Gradually it was decided to study the influence on the treatment relationship of racial differences between workers and clients. The problems inherent in such a study are obvious; although reality factors prevented its completion, there is little doubt that the complexity of the task may have doomed the study to failure. The experience, however, laid the foundation for staff dialogue on racism, and a description of this abortive effort may be of general interest.

It was postulated that (1) workers and clients of different races experience unique transference and countertransference complications as they engage in treatment, and (2) it is necessary to understand and deal with these complications if treatment is to be successful on more than a superficial level. The study group consisted of four experienced social workers—two blacks and two whites.[6] The writer, then a part-time staff member, served as coordinator. At the close of each case in which the worker and client were of different races, the workers were asked to complete a schedule that was designed to elicit manifestations of transference and countertransference as detected by the workers. The study was terminated in its beginning stages when two of the workers left the agency for professional reasons. At that time the participants were convinced that the approach could prove fruitful.

A retrospective analysis of the experience leads to the conclusion that this approach to racism through practice research was premature. Although it held promise of gain on one level, it was sadly limited in other more significant respects. Designed to approach the problem on an emotional level, its methods were primarily intellectual. The sharing within the study group of insights into transference and countertransference in biracial situations did serve a useful purpose, however, for it increased the participants' awareness of the need to cope with subtle forms of racism that affect services to clients.

The termination of this study effort without the achievement of any real degree of closure was disturbing to the participants, who were left with feelings of hopelessness.[7] Its more useful by-products were overlooked until a renewed effort to gain even minimal closure resulted in the development of a more productive approach to the problem.[8]

Staff dialogue

In the fall of 1970, the two remaining study participants agreed to join with the writer in an effort to distill something meaningful from the aborted study in order to share it with the staff. It was fortunate that many other current demands led to a decision to undertake this distillation without formal planning by the participants. In retrospect it is believed that this condition resulted in a spontaneous shift from the intellectual to the feeling level and thus laid a meaningful foundation for the staff dialogue that ensued.

During this period, the agency was engaging in major changes in its administrative patterns, and regular staff meetings were devoted to these changes. The presentation of the aborted research effort was therefore scheduled as an extra session during a lunch hour, and an invitation was issued to those who were interested in hearing the "report." The response appears to indicate the felt needs of the staff. More than forty of the fifty-three staff members attended the first session. The interest level was high, and the session ended with a decision to have a second meeting in two weeks.

From the opening reporting session on October 14, 1970, until the planned termination on February 23, 1971, several significant phases in the process may be identified. The first stage, a period that included three biweekly sessions, was characterized by intellectualization on the part of both black and white staff members. There was a strong tendency to adhere to the use of repressive mechanisms as a means of avoiding both the individual and institutional racism repre-sented in the group. In some ways, the group process could be said to recapitulate the history of black-white relation-ships in society.

A second phase was entered when the group saw the need to decide whether to pursue the issue on a more meaningful level or to discontinue the meetings. During the fourth and fifth sessions there was controlled confrontation between white and black workers, and many aspects of racism were brought to the fore. The group agreed that the dialogue had existed primarily on an intellectual level. The general tenor of the early sessions is reflected in the follow-ing instance.

There had been a staff party at which square dancing was the featured activity. Although the occasion was not well attended in general, few black staff members were present. In the session immediately following this event, which took place between the first and second meetings, some white workers expressed concern that black staff had participated only minimally in this social occasion. Their remarks led to a minor confrontation.

Black workers accused the white workers of asking inappropriate questions about what they did on their own time and noted that the white staff did not ask whites why they had not attended. The hostile interchange that took place was quickly smoothed over by the group in an effort to re-create a semblance of harmony and good will.

Following this interchange, black workers expressed their disillusionment with the effort and indicated that the sessions, as they were, were not worth an investment of time. What was generally overlooked was that some participants were experiencing this kind of interchange for the first time and that, for a number of black and white people, an intellectual approach was a necessary preamble.

The third phase began during the fifth session, December 16, 1970, when the group decided to have a series of eight sessions to be held at weekly rather than biweekly intervals, scheduled at "prime" agency time rather than during lunch hours.[9] It was later decided to issue an invitation to the total social work staff, thus not limiting the series to those who had attended the first five sessions. At the same time it was decided that those who chose to be present for the opening session on January 4, 1971, were entering into a general agreement to involve themselves for the series of eight sessions. If the desired goals were to be reached, it seemed advisable to eliminate the possibility of people dropping in and interfering with the group process.

These decisions resulted in some dropouts, several of whom were part-time staff members who questioned the desirability of their involvement because of the time that would have to be expended. As a result thirty-three persons, all of whom had been involved in the first phases, became the participants in the eight-session series.

Content and process

The group agreed immediately that these sessions would be productive only if there were a successful departure from intellectualization to communication on a feeling level. A first attempt was made when the participants began to recollect early experiences with persons of the opposite race. They had apparently gained sufficient comfort during the first two phases of group development to share some of the pain, bitterness, anguish, and frustration of early life encounters. Much of the content was highly emotional, and at times both individual and group equilibrium seemed threatened by the impact.[10]

A young black woman described her parents' reactions and the closeness that developed within the family and within the community following the "accidental" killing of a black neighbor by a white man. A young black man spoke of his mother's experience as a day worker in white homes and of how he felt about wearing secondhand clothing from those homes. A black case aide shared her personal experiences as a maid in the home of a middle-class white family.

A young white man pointed out that, in the environment in which he had grown up, manhood was considered not fully achieved until the white male had cohabited with a black woman. Another young man told how a generally accepted outlet for restlessness or frustration in white youth in his small town was riding with a group of boys through the black community and throwing rocks. A young white woman described a moment in her childhood when, following a spontaneous expression of affection for a black maid, she was told by her mother that she must never kiss a black person.

The first two sessions of the series, in which such emotionally charged experiences were shared, were followed by a partial retreat to the intellectual level. An air of hopelessness and discouragement permeated the group as this development occurred, and several persons directly expressed their feelings of depression. When individual and group anxiety was handled either by emotional withdrawal or intellectualization, some of the black staff members stated in various ways that they should have known better than to expect anything else. Their disappointment and anger bewildered many white workers who believed that they were making a genuine effort to deal with their own racism, which, by this time, they were no longer denying.

It seems safe to say that by the midpoint in the series the first major objective—loosening the repressive psychological mechanisms—had been accomplished. At this time the participants were understandably concerned about how to handle the rampant anxiety that had been unleashed. The brief retreat to intellectualization as a means of coping with this anxiety was not on an abstract level as it had been previously but entailed a need for action. Confrontation became more direct and more honest. Anger and frustration were identified as common emotions held by both black and white staff. Although at times it was hard to locate, a thread of hope still appeared to run through the sessions, and threats to give up were not carried out.

In the last few sessions the theme of separatism began to emerge, and at times this theme threatened to overwhelm those participants who tended to view separatism as another form of racism or as white racism in reverse. White staff began to confront blacks with accusations of reverse racism. This stage of the dialogue was short-lived. To their credit, most of the white workers had the courage to face the overwhelming impact of the reality that the distribution of power in society spawns the development of white but not black racism. Although it was not specifically stated in group discussions, the participants' understanding of racism appeared to shift from the dictionary definition to a more relevant interpretation:

> . . . the predication of decisions and policies on considerations of race for the purpose of *subordinating* a racial group and maintaining control over that group. . . . It takes two . . . forms . . . individual racism and institutional racism.[11]

Group awakening to the implications of this interpretation produced heightened anxiety. A subtle shift from the more manageable struggle with individual racism to the overwhelming aspects of institutional racism had taken place. The writer, carrying the leadership role, undertook to redirect the group to cope more fully with individual racism as the foundation of institutional racism. The working premise here is well stated by Barbara Shannon in her significant article on the implications of racism for social work.

> The importance of economics and education must not be minimized, but it is only through the individual that racism can be eradicated. Given a pyramidal hierarchy of societal organization, the individual is at the bottom, with the second and third levels being groups (including the family) and institutions respectively. Institutional racism will not disappear until individuals change, because no pyramid has ever been razed by destroying its tip.[12]

Dialogue on individual racism reached a level of honesty that had not been attained in earlier sessions. Some black workers who recognized that they had handled black-white relationships by general acceptance of the white world's approach to integration shifted to a clearer alignment with black staff members who had no faith in this approach. Their courage in taking this step and in sharing their feelings with the group left no individual participant untouched. Grief became a common denominator. Dialogue, because it requires language and is dependent on cognitive processes, diminished in usefulness.

Group participants—both black and white and in varying degrees and for varying reasons—struggled with the ambivalence that accompanied the termination of the scheduled sessions. The relative safety of biracial group dialogue had to be given up, and the uncertainty about what would replace it stimulated additional anxiety. Would it be informal dialogue, individual to individual without regard to race, or should there be planned dialogue on a separatist level, with whites talking with whites and blacks with blacks?[13]

Movement toward planning future steps was curtailed by the group itself. The experience of "gut-level" sharing appeared to support the participants in warding off the natural tendency to settle once again for superficial harmony. By common agreement individual and group anxiety were left at a level that held promise of being a mobilizing rather than an impeding force in the eradication of the residuals of racism in the participants. The general drift of thought and feeling was reflected in the closing session.

A young black man who had openly shared his personal experiences with racism indicated that he had reached the point of no longer being willing to engage in this kind of sharing. He expressed his opinion that continuation of the biracial dialogue placed an inordinate demand on him as a black person and that not only should he not be expected to pay the price but he questioned whether any further purpose could be served through such sharing. He thought the time had come for whites to "deal with the mess they had created."

This position, which he expressed in various ways throughout the session, was supported by other blacks. The young man had emerged as a leader among the others, and his softly spoken comments became serious pronouncements that penetrated intellectual defenses and affected the participants on a feeling level. The interchange, which was highly emotional in quality, reached a new level of honesty. Group members, both black and white, were able to support each other, even across racial lines, in terminating at this time. The dialogue closed as the young man quietly observed, "I think it's time to go."

Evaluation

Planned staff dialogue appears to be a useful approach to racism when the participants, although at various stages in their own resolution of black-white issues, share a common concern about the implications of racism for the profession.

The approach, as it was developed by this particular staff, served to loosen the repressive psychological mechanisms that are at work in some form in most individuals and that have been institutionalized in the social work profession. The major objective of the dialogue, that of loosening the mechanisms and gaining fuller access to the problem on a feeling level, was reached. Its achievement disclosed other objectives that were beyond the scope of this endeavor.

It has been noted that the group participants—probably without exception—experienced intense pain and had to cope with anguish, frustration, anger, and depression. Some persons who began the dialogue feeling free of racism discovered troubling residuals within themselves. It is noteworthy, in this regard, that no one acted as if he were superior to anyone else and that each individual appeared to cope with the problem as it existed for him. The honesty of the participants was impressive. The sharing of painful insights in so large a group requires courage and a climate of common concern.[14]

Prologue to action?

A prologue is a "preliminary act or course of action foreshadowing greater events."[15] Was the described dialogue a prologue to greater events? Implicit in stating that it was a prologue is the recognition that the dialogue was a form of action and not simply an engrossing conversation. When the writer figuratively took the pulse of the group, the reading suggested that the individuals were experiencing the gratification that comes primarily from a sense of doing something about a problem. During the earlier stages, when the involvement was primarily intellectual, the reading showed the frustration that is the usual by-product of just talking. A final reading, during the last session, indicated that there was at least a blending of gratification—the result of having engaged in a form of action—frustration, and disappointment in the action's being so limited.

The final session was highly charged emotionally because of the frustration and disappointment. The natural inclination to settle disturbed and conflicting feelings was successfully avoided in favor of ending the dialogue where the participants as human beings really were, that is, hurt, frightened, depressed but, at the same time, clearer about the need for this experience to be truly a prologue to greater events.[16]

Notes

1. Editorial Notes, *Social Casework*, 45:155 (March 1964).

2. Child Service and Family Counseling Center, Atlanta, Georgia.

3. Racism is defined as racialism, "a doctrine or feeling of racial differences or antagonisms, especially with reference to supposed racial superiority, inferiority, or purity; racial prejudice, hatred, or discrimination"; see *Webster's New Twentieth Century Dictionary*, s.v. "racism."

4. The following articles are of interest: Julia B. Bloch, The White Worker and the Negro Client in Psychotherapy, *Social Work*, 13:36–42 (April 1968); Jerome Cohen, Race as a Factor in Social Work Practice, in *Race, Research, and Reason: Social Work Perspectives*, ed. Roger R. Miller (New York: National Association of Social Workers, 1969), pp. 99–113; Andrew E. Curry, The Negro Worker and the White Client: A Commentary on the Treatment Relationship, *Social Casework*, 45:131–36 (March 1964); Esther Fibush, The White Worker and the Negro Client, *Social Casework*, 46:271–77 (May 1965); Esther Fibush and BeAlva Turnquest, A Black and White Approach to the Problem of Racism, *Social Casework*, 51:459–66 (October 1970); Jean S. Gochros, Recognition and Use of Anger in Negro Clients, *Social Work*, 11:28–34 (January 1966); Seaton W. Manning, Cultural and Value Factors Affecting the Negro's Use of Agency Services, *Social Work*, 5:3–13 (October 1960); Donald E. Meeks, The White Ego Ideal: Implications for the Bi-Racial Treatment Relationship, *Smith College Studies in Social Work*, 37:93–105 (February 1967); Barbara E. Shannon, Implications of White Racism for Social Work Practice, *Social Casework*, 51:270–76 (May 1970); Leonard C. Simmons, "Crow Jim": Implications for Social Work, *Social Work*, 8:24–30 (July 1963); and Margaret Weiner, Gentlemen's Agreement Revisited, *Social Casework*, 51:395–98 (July 1970).

5. The Family Counseling Center of Metropolitan Atlanta and the Children's Center of Metropolitan Atlanta merged to form the present Child Service and Family Counseling Center in 1969.

6. The social workers were Diane Abernathy, Genevieve Hill, Millie Kagan, and Victoria Scott.

7. Toward the end of the time period in which this study was taking place, the agency became a participant in the National Experiment in Staff Development (NESD) II, a two-and-one-half-year program funded by the National Institute of Mental Health, in which five member agencies of Family Service Association of America participated. The ten staff members involved in this project selected as their focus the impact of urbanization on the black family and the agency's responsibility for becoming "relevant" in its services to the black urban poor. From this specific concern there was a natural drift toward consideration of the effects of individual and institutional racism on the provision of services. This stage in the NESD II group coincided with a period of disquietude that was being experienced by the participants in the study group. The influence of the NESD II effort on subsequent developments is difficult to assess. Whereas the NESD group's work on racism was a planned, organized effort, the staff dialogue was "grass roots" in character.

8. Mary Margaret Carr, director of the agency, is responsible for keeping the issue open. Without persistence on her part it seems likely that inappropriate closure may have been reached.

9. This change presented a scheduling problem. The most feasible time for the dialogue was the period scheduled for biweekly consultations on group treatment with Dr. Sidney Isenberg. The group suggested that he be invited to join as a participant. Thereafter, beginning with the second of the eight-session series, Dr. Isenberg was present and was of invaluable assistance. The writer is a teacher by preparation and experience, and the difficult role shift to group leader and enabler was made less problematic by Dr. Isenberg's involvement.

10. It should be noted that neither the majority of the participants, nor the leader, wanted this experience to become that of an encounter or sensitivity group. The size of the group provided a natural safeguard against such a development.

11. Stokely Carmichael and Charles V. Hamilton, *Black Power: The Politics of Liberation in America* (New York: Random House, Vintage Books, 1967), pp. 3–4.

12. Shannon, Implications of White Racism, p. 272.

13. For a useful discussion of the sharing of feelings about black-white relationships on a one-to-one basis, see Fibush and Turnquest, Approach to the Problems of Racism.

14. Although the size of the group undoubtedly inhibited some participants, it also served to protect them. Everyone became a participant, whether verbally or nonverbally, and those who preferred to work on their concerns in silence were allowed the appropriate privacy.

15. *Webster's New Twentieth Century Dictionary,* s.v. "prologue."

16. Following the preparation of this article for publication—in essence the recounting of staff involvement in working on individual racism—the NESD II group planned and sponsored a two-day "live-in" workshop on individual racism in which approximately one hundred staff and board members were involved. Prior to the workshop, May 6 and 7, 1971, there was a four-session series of dialogue for staff who had not attended the eight-session series described in this article. These sessions were primarily preparatory for the workshop on racism.

RELEVANT AGENCY PROGRAMS FOR THE URBAN COMMUNITY

Howard Hush, Joseph H. Kahle, Joseph McDonald,
and Edwin F. Watson

The authors of the following four articles comprised a panel for a session on November 17, 1969, of the Family Service Association of America Biennial Meeting. The meeting was held in Philadelphia, Pennsylvania, November 16–19, 1969.

Howard Hush

In the past few years, Family Service of Metropolitan Detroit has taken steps to become more representative of the urban community it serves. Every effort has been made to recruit black staff members, both professional and clerical. The agency's board, too, has become more representative of the community. Various religious persuasions are represented, management and labor are represented, the poor (that is the

Reprinted from *Social Casework*, April 1970.

fairly poor) are represented, clients are represented, and, of course, both the black community and the white community are represented. Some board members know from experience what the inner city is all about right now; there are others, however, whose knowledge of discrimination, poverty, and family disorganization is based entirely upon hearsay.

In order to reach those members of the community—the black, the poor, the deprived, the isolated—who had not previously been served to the same extent, the agency initiated special programs and services. An Emergency Counseling Service was established three years ago for the specific purpose of reaching families and individuals in one area of the inner city, and an experimental family life education program designed to reach the same segment of the community has been launched. According to the statistics, these programs have been successful. In 1968, for example, 47 percent of the agency's clientele were black in a service area that is only 22 percent black. The median family income of those served was $6,500, as compared with $7,500 for the area. Thirty percent of the families served had annual incomes of less than $5,000.

Facts like these that seem to have escaped the attention of a hardy breed of dedicated critics—who keep telling us that the voluntary family service agency is concerned only with white, middle-class suburban families and their sophisticated, well-nourished tensions—are not unusual. Nevertheless, family agencies in urban communities are still asking such questions as, How much impact are we really having? Do we have—have we ever had—the power to bring about significant change? Forgetting all other questions for the time being, where do we go from here? What do we do next? I have the following three suggestions to offer, none of which is original: (1) find out what black people are saying, (2) discard some of the older assumptions under which we have operated in the past, and (3) produce more than grandiose rhetoric in the field of social action.

Most of us face an enormous task of self-education if we

are to understand and serve the black community; it is no longer enough to be a political liberal. Because, in my judgment, the problem is personal for most of us, I know of no way to make my first point without being personal.

I grew up in rural Iowa, which was and still is about as white as white can be. I went to a high school that had two black students (out of 375) neither of whom I ever knew. I attended one of the most liberal of liberal arts colleges in the Middle West with an enrollment of 675 students, two of whom were black and only one of whom I knew. I was educated from—or indoctrinated by, some will say—the same textbooks available to most of you. My political upbringing was indeed liberal; in fact, some of our neighbors thought we were dangerously liberal.

About three years ago, as a result of my agency experience, I began to sense in a deeply personal way the gap between rural white Iowa, which I had left in the thirties, and the black urban areas of the sixties. I began to feel confusion about and impatience with the spreading concept of black nationalism. Because of my own curiosity and the warm interest in my reeducation by a few black staff members, I increased my reading of books by black authors.

I began with James Baldwin's *The Fire Next Time*, a remarkable description of what it really feels like to be black in a white society. Next came Dick Gregory's *Nigger*, an earthy, gripping account of life on public assistance and his struggle to become the man we know today. Then there was Franz Fanon's *The Wretched of the Earth*, a scholarly historical account of black frustration and black-white conflict in an African setting; it is heavy going, but it is basic material. I went on to Martin Luther King's *Where Do We Go From Here?*, a beautiful statement but, in retrospect, maybe too gentle.

About this time one of my sympathetic staff members suggested that I read a novel by John Williams entitled *The Man Who Cried I Am*. Being over thirty, I got through this one but only by constantly reminding myself that it had to do with race instead of sex, a subject that is said to be closely related to race. Then came the *Autobiography of Malcolm X,* which brought me the greatest shock, not because of the content but because of the misconception I had built up over the years about the man, his life, and his cause. Most recently I read Dr. Nathan Wright's book entitled *Let's Work Together,* a rational, forthright statement of the racial dilemma that suggests courses of action for white people.

These books have a common theme of black frustration, reflecting the outpourings of very competent writers, all of whom are black. I cannot say specifically how my own attitude and performance will ultimately be affected by these readings, but I do think that anyone who is identified in a responsible way with a family agency—or any agency—in an urban community these days should discover what these blacks are saying. If we are not acquainted with these writers and their writings, or if we can read these books without being shaken by the impact of the message, I am not sure we are prepared by experience or personal qualifications to be in leadership positions in family service agencies.

I should like to make a few brash comments on the old question of service coverage by family agencies in urban areas, a question that poses a serious problem for many of us.

It is reasonably accurate, but of course oversimplified, to say that historically those of us in family service agencies have promoted or allowed to thrive some views that are no longer relevant to the current scene. These older assumptions can be summarized as follows: (1) the family is the basic institution in our society; (2) the family service agency is the community agency to serve the family; (3) most families with relationship problems can best be served by a family service agency; (4) with adequate financing, family agencies could—and should—provide the basic service to most families suffering from relationship stress; and (5) family agencies should be regarded as the focal point of community expertise and action with respect to the family.

Instead of adhering strictly to these older views, it would

be more realistic for family agencies in most urban areas today to be guided by the following considerations.

1. We do not have a monopoly of concern and expertise with the family, being only one of a great number and variety of community groups interested in the family as an institution. Neither have we established our own unique contribution in this picture, and it serves little purpose to pretend that we have.

2. With respect to financing, I see no prospect that we will be recognized and financed as *the* family service for troubled families. In my agency the ratio of practicing caseworkers in family counseling to population is 1 to 100,000, which is a ridiculous ratio. During the past two years, in the face of record family breakdown and an enormous amount of public rhetoric expressing concern for the family, we, like many other family agencies, have had to curtail service. I see no prospect of any dramatic breakthrough in the financing of family service in the next three to five years.

3. The public commitment to the family as an institution is shifting, uncertain, and reluctant. We have used the family to develop the rationale for our being as family agencies. Yet somehow the public is not now generally impressed. It is more likely to be impressed by such groupings as youth, the aging, the minority group, the neighborhood group, and the handicapped. Ironically, the family as an institution seems to be without much appeal these days. To many people the family is a shadowy kind of institution, blurred in its outline by clichés and platitudes, by statistics of failure, and by commercial flaunting of traditional values; some have a deep personal awareness of the family as a less-than-perfect institution.

Since we do not now have family counseling service under our auspices on a coverage basis, and since we cannot realistically aspire to it in the next five years or so, what do we do? Where and how do we apply our expertise? How do we justify our claim upon the community's dollar?

Even though my agency is allocating 80 percent of its program dollar to direct work with families and individuals (and I am not necessarily suggesting that this percentage is too high), we are restless and bewildered by the thin service coverage. We are therefore exploring other ways to use our expertise that provide a different kind of payoff. Following are two illustrations, both of which have stirred up new interest in and controversy about our program.

Early in the summer of 1969, the Michigan Bell Telephone Company came to us with a problem and a proposition. The company had employed hundreds of inner-city young women as operators. Most of them were poor, black, and generally deprived; they usually had no work experience and had not completed high school. The on-the-job problems the women presented were enormous, and management-supervisory personnel were not able to communicate with them without provoking hostility and poor job performance. The company asked us to develop and lead, over a two-month period, a series of experimental seminars with a small group of management-supervisory personnel that would give them a better understanding of the operators and the kinds of community and family life they had known.

The company assumed that we knew something about the stresses of families and individuals, and it was ready to pay us for our expertise. (It was, of course, the offer to pay that threw us into a panic.) We welcomed the opportunity to test the usefulness of our knowledge and skill in a different setting, to demonstrate that our talents have value and are worth stronger community support, and to help hundreds of deprived young women in the inner city to achieve some success in the area of employment. At present the experimental series of seminars has been completed, and we have made a joint assessment of it with the Michigan Bell Telephone Company. The assessment was most favorable, and a second series of seminars was planned for the spring of 1970 with a different group of management-supervisory personnel.

The other program that deviates from our traditional family counseling approach is being conducted in the public schools.[1] Briefly, it was begun in 1967 and is a training program to assist teachers with differing academic and social backgrounds in developing effective family life classes.

Although the activities described here are not family counseling in the traditional sense, they do represent a use of whatever knowledge and expertise we may have developed from our experience in working with families. Who is to say that in the long run this kind of activity has more, or less, impact upon family life than some of the other activities of the past twenty years or so? We do not know, but we believe it might be useful to find out.

The other panelists will be commenting on social action or advocacy. I am sure that their comments will produce something more than grandiose rhetoric on what we as voluntary agencies can actually do effectively in this field. I think we must be as realistic here as I have tried to suggest we need to be with respect to service coverage by a family service agency in an urban area.

Joseph H. Kahle

To use an overworked term, all family service agencies are concerned with keeping their services "relevant" to the needs of the people in the communities they serve. For some time we have been hearing about advocacy as one of the functions we must undertake if we are to relate our services to problems arising from the crises stemming from the complications of living in an urbanized environment. Advocacy is not a new responsibility of family service agencies. Effective family advocacy is a vital role of the family service agency and one with which we are not yet prepared to deal.

Advocacy, either expressed or implied, has been the responsibility of family service agencies since their inception. All workers in our agencies have, to some extent, played the role of advocate at one time or another. The fact that FSAA must now design a special program to recognize formally our responsibility for advocacy confirms how far we have drifted from our original purpose. In the early days, family service set forth to improve family life and the conditions under which families lived.

The early histories of many of the older family service agencies provide numerous instances of board members who crusaded for better living, employment, education, and welfare conditions for the poor. Somewhere along the line that crusading spark diminished. The emphasis shifted from improving social conditions to treating social pathology. For many reasons we let ourselves be diverted into becoming specialists in treating individual and family dysfunctioning, and for a long time we have directed most of our efforts toward the comfortable, introspective process of social casework. As a national federation of agencies, we have accepted casework as the "core service" of our agencies. Only in recent years have many of us begun to realize that we cannot concentrate only on a single social work method.

In the pamphlet, *Range and Emphases of a Family Service Program,* published by FSAA in 1963, we were reminded again of our second function—"improving the social environment." We have allowed ourselves to believe that we are carrying out our share of the community's responsibility for improving the environment by serving on committees, developing programs of family life and education, making speeches supporting the traditional values of family life, and, very occasionally and very cautiously, challenging some of the community's cherished but misdirected values. Now we have to face the probability that casework, educating families, participating in community studies, and interminable hours of talk are not enough to help many of the people with whom we work.

In many cities the family service agency is the only general purpose agency available to all the citizens. Because family agencies have such broadly varied service programs, they tend to be the recipients of the end products of society's defective systems. We receive the products of an outmoded, ineffectual educational system that ill prepares our young people for the world. We receive the products of a dehumanizing welfare system which has completely failed to carry out its designated functions. We receive the people cast aside by our economic system as misfits. We receive the failures of our health and mental health systems, and we are asked to help these people to adjust to these systems—an impossible job. Yet, many family agencies have welcomed that impossible job, convinced that they can treat these untreatable situations. When they fail, it is fashionable to blame the client and say that the failure occurred because of his lack of motivation—not because the agency or worker has failed to recognize that the systems are at fault and need to change, or that the agencies must try to change them.

Time and the community's tolerance for our agencies' efforts have almost run out, as is perhaps indicated by the shrinking of many of our agencies' budgets and the opinions of the poor and of racial minority groups in our communities. If our programs are to be really significant, we must stop working in the past and start working with present conditions. For our programs to be related to the needs of our clients, we must reach far beyond the present concept of casework to dealing with some of the factors that defeat people. We must try to make society's defective systems serve the needs of the people rather than their own internal needs or the needs of special interest groups. We must use a wide variety of methods and skills, and we must use what we learn from our clients about the way the systems work or fail.

We must learn something from business and industry about systems analysis. Without such knowledge we will be unable to bring about social change. There is considerable knowledge about industrial and military systems, but little is known about social systems and how they work. One of our first jobs in undertaking a commitment to family advocacy is to learn as much as we can about the organization and function of the various social systems with which we deal most frequently.

Being an advocate for clients is a professional responsibility for every social worker, not just for those who work in family service agencies. In this regard, I disagree with the

FSAA's proposal, as it was first written, that agencies employ or designate one or two staff members as family advocates. Each board member and volunteer must either himself be an advocate or be firmly committed to advocacy as an agency function and responsibility, as agencies will discover when they develop programs of advocacy. To place the important responsibility for community advocacy in the hands of one or two staff members is merely a token gesture toward improving the social environment.

There are two basic forms of advocacy: family advocacy and community advocacy. The family advocate has the responsibility of acting as a representative for an individual client or family. At times, he may have to fight their battles with the systems for them, if they cannot; and if they have the capability, his job is to show them how to fight their own battles effectively. He may spend part of his time helping a client to fight his way through the red tape of a welfare application; or at a juvenile court hearing, helping his client preserve his rights; or helping him battle against educators to allow an unruly but educable child to reenter a public school; or intervening on a client's behalf when a recalcitrant intern or clerk prevents his getting service at a hospital. This is true family advocacy.

The FSAA proposal is concerned with community advocacy. In this type of advocacy program, the agency is referring to large segments of the community. From our knowledge and experience gained from working with large numbers of people, we come to see the need to change the monolithic, defeating systems affecting our clients' lives. This form of advocacy should not be carried out by any single staff or board member; it requires the collective action of the agency, board, and staff, perhaps in cooperation with other agencies. Community advocacy requires analysis of the system to be changed, planning for the strategies to be employed, and a thorough consideration of the effects upon the agency and the community of any action undertaken. One of the strategies to be used might involve stimulating collective action on the part of client groups toward changing a particular system. Such an action by an agency cannot be undertaken impulsively and without a thorough understanding of the possible results on the agency's future effectiveness.

As I have already indicated, being an advocate requires commitment and active involvement of staff and board members. We must be prepared on occasion to "lay it on the line" when it really counts, and not just when it is safe. We must be able to anticipate the reaction to an unpopular cause and the overall results on the continuing effectiveness of our agency.

With the adoption and formal recognition of advocacy as an important part of our agencies' programs, we are in a way returning to the days of Jane Addams and Hull House, when social work was largely devoted to improving the environment. I am not implying that we should discard casework as a means of helping our clients. Instead, I am suggesting that we combine the casework method, the knowledge that we have gained from the experiences of our clients, and the two forms of advocacy I have outlined. By providing this combination of services, we will help our clients more than we have before.

The modern family service agency requires skillful and mature staff. Many of us have concluded that the need today is not for the traditional caseworker, but for the generic or multifunctional social worker now being trained by some of the schools of social work. This worker must be skilled in the variety of necessary client-focused services, such as community advocacy, planning, and community action. The new breed of social worker finds the variety of the functions of his assignment stimulating and exciting. He develops an active commitment to his clients and to the community rather than the routine commitment which we have been accused of having.

The family agency really has no choice in whether it will or will not commit itself to advocacy as one of its functions. Without such a commitment, we are only partially serving our clients and the community. Our present knowledge and experience justify this conclusion—that we must not ignore or we will fail to carry out our responsibilities for improving the social environment.

Joseph McDonald

Our objective in this presentation is not to supply firm answers, but rather to give some idea from a local vantage point of how we have been struggling to deal with problems concerning poverty and racial discrimination.

Two months before rebellion in the streets hit Cincinnati, I offered a special report to my board of directors. I predicted that there would be violence and that it was not far off. My forecast was based on the fact that Cincinnati's total efforts—by our agency, by other agencies, by government, by business, by the churches, by the community generally—to deal with the double problem of poverty and racial discrimination added up to mere tokenism. The board was quick to agree with this analysis. In fact, board members seemed relieved to have these views out in the open. Apparently some people had sensed the superficial response to anguish and anger, but they did not know whether it was true and, if so, how to deal with it.

I further suggested that as a result of their voicelessness, poor black people would seek militant voices to speak for them. These spokesmen would not, as in the past, be chosen by others. They would be independent, following only their own bidding. Many of our staff and board agreed that racial conflict is indeed the number one issue of our day. Many agreed with the finding of the President's Commission on Civil Disorders that our whole system is based on racism. Board and staff concurred that we did not know our black community. We set out to educate and inform ourselves by extensive reading and listening. We initiated a number of special meetings for both board and staff, sometimes inviting guests from such organizations as the Community Chest. To these meetings we continue to invite local and outside guest speakers—mainly black.

Immediately after the first wave of riots in our community, we invited groups of clients who lived in areas where there was the greatest violence to come in and tell us exactly what had happened and its effect on their families and offer their suggestions for solution. We heard from two groups of adults, parents in the main, and one group of young people, and what they told us was really shocking. Each of these meetings was attended by two members of the board, myself, one other administrative staff member, and approximately ten to fifteen client guests. There were no comforting answers to the questions that we sometimes asked hopefully.

I am convinced that we learn more from actual personal exposure than from reading and listening. We found that the term *black power* is a useful equivalent for self-belief, for self-power, and for self-direction by black people. We found this concept helpful in understanding the phenomena associated with racial conflict.

Dr. Nathan Wright, Jr., prominent writer, civil rights leader and educator, now on the faculty of The State University of New York at Albany, served as key consultant in our re-orientation. During a series of meetings we had a considerable and often discomforting interchange of ideas. One of these meetings was held on an evening when people were not permitted on the streets because of violence following Martin Luther King's assassination.

Subsequently, our casework practice has been going through some adaptations. We have become involved in work with neighborhood centers, in new forms of collaboration, in a complete change of the use of our family life education program, and in other new priorities which I cannot explain in detail here. I do, however, want to mention some notions from professional experience that I feel we need to revise.

We have always been for integration. Why should we urge integration unless it is our own integration? Agencies would be less controlling if they promoted desegregation. Let the black man decide when he is ready to integrate. If he does not want to integrate immediately, it is his business.

Equality has been a popular idea, but unlike equity, it only implies equal opportunity to vie for the same goals. Why should the other fellow have to accept my goals? Espousing equity, freedom to choose one's own goals, is more consistent with self-realization.

Social agencies have been great believers in the demonstration of new services. Serious reconsideration of this business of demonstrating services reveals that it frequently is an excuse for imposing one's own ideas and solutions.

We have held firmly to a belief that good casework is color-blind. I suggest that this is something of a white myth. Our family caseworkers who have recognized racial differences directly with their clients have found that they got further than when they denied these differences.

Our agencies—in fact our whole society—give priority to children's needs. There are many reasons for this, some of them sound, but some perhaps convenient excuses for giving up on helping the adult whose own pattern of adequacy —no matter how angry he now may be at society—is a more important model for his child than anything that someone else offers.

Our goals very often have been toward ameliorating problems. Why have we not offered more support of self-assertion and self-realization, although they may be anything but ameliorative from a short-range point of view? By providing outposts and otherwise making agency services more accessible in their present form, we have expected that more blacks would turn to us for counseling. This expectation, too, I suggest we should review more realistically.

Our agency board has been groping for a new role in social action. The sincerity of our attempts through the years to improve welfare by legislation cannot be doubted, but these efforts on public issues have not averted a net loss of ground.

Now we are trying to give more backing to responsible

people within the neighborhoods, to stop misunderstanding and even subverting each new effort and evidence of self-power, self-assertion, and self-determination. We have, in small ways, earned some trust from some of our black neighborhood leaders, and we are being invited quietly, but increasingly, to play a broker's role between some of them and parts of the larger community that either does not understand them or has not listened.

We have been asked, for instance, for help in dealing with zoning problems resulting from routine hearings and decisions that push people out of changing neighborhoods. We were asked for help in dealing with a huge hospital whose services are totally unavailable to the people in its surrounding impoverished neighborhood. Recently we were invited to help open channels of communication with developers who have been evicting families in order to convert property to more lucrative uses. We were asked to bring in some of the employment people from the National Association of Businessmen so that Office of Economic Opportunity leaders could tell them some of the things that are not being accomplished, despite rosy statistics.

This path is uncertain and even hazardous. We have had doors slammed in our faces. We are by no means always successful, and I would not lead you to believe that we are assured immunity from black anger. Recently a neighborhood newspaper ran a page one editorial entitled, "Do Something, Damn It." It took to task every institution in the neighborhood where our headquarters is located but did not mention our agency—which we accepted as a vote of confidence.

Because this course must defer credit and publicity to others, we have no guarantee that the "establishment" will understand or support us for this kind of action. We are sure, however, that if we claimed credit on our own we would jeopardize our trusting relationship. Nevertheless, we are convinced that this method will assist us to be more responsive and helpful to our whole community. We *have* stopped wasting time trying to explain why the black community should not be angry with us. We *are* trying!

Edwin F. Watson

I have been asked to discuss program needs and goals of the family service agency in the large urban area. In particular, I intend to stress organizational attitudes toward changing priorities and developing new service capabilities that are necessary for innovation in response to contemporary needs.

The Toronto agency has been through an extensive self-examination during the past year and a half. We called it a direction of service study. It represents an effort by the agency at all levels—staff, board, and committees—to re-examine our position in relation to service directions for the community we serve. What was needed—and what the report of the study attempted to do—was to set forth what seemed to be relevant operating assumptions and to use these as guidelines by which to chart broad program directions and to begin to establish some new priorities.

These assumptions can be summarized as follows:

1. Family Service Association should *continue* to provide and improve services that are relevant to the needs of both individuals and families within Metropolitan Toronto.

2. Family Service Association should strive to make these services as accessible as possible to the people it serves. Accessibility is more than geographic proximity. It encompasses reaching out to those individuals and groups who are most vulnerable to personal, social, and community stresses.

3. Family Service Association, in the light of its observations of the *dynamic interplay* among individuals and their families and their surrounding society, must add to its means of intervention by broadening or acquiring different methods of reaching people and serving their needs appropriately.

4. Family Service Association should strive to incorporate within itself an innovative capability which would place its philosophy, current program commitments, organization, and administration under consistent review, adaptation, and renewal.

5. Family Service Association should give high priority to services to those individuals and families who are most

vulnerable within the social structure. Family Service Association's concern for and contribution to the "greater social health of the community" should grow out of its expanding experience with these individuals and families. The agency's preventive and social action commitments should also flow from this involvement with and service to those sectors of the population that are subject to the greatest social hazards.

6. The agency's program should reflect the dynamic interrelationship between the individual and the society or community. It is inadequate to regard personal or social problems as the result of individual pathology. Future programming must reflect fuller understanding of both individual personality *and* prevailing environmental conditions. Although this idea is not original, it is now a social fact of much significance.

7. Family Service Association reaffirms its aim to assist the individual and the community toward a maximum degree of self-help and self-realization, as far as these are consistent with the realities of our social interdependence as human beings. For Family Service Association's program, intensive short-term service to individuals and communities should be creatively used to increase capacities for self-help. The development of community supports to sustain individuals, families, and communities in maximum independence is equally necessary.

These "operating assumptions" are suggestions for future planning of agency services, but in no sense are they meant to be a prescription or a solution. All of them contain implications which are significant in the implementation of program objectives. Inevitably, they raise difficult matters of choice and decision, but they represent a clear shift from an agency focused on social work *methods* to an agency focused on *social problems* in which the methods employed by the staff are seen as an outgrowth of the issues or problems toward which they may direct their energies and resources.

One may ask what the impact of these general mandates for

innovation and change has been. In the course of the study, the staff and resources of the Toronto agency shifted significantly from approximately 90 percent involvement in individual casework and family therapy to about 60 percent, with about 40 percent devoted to community-oriented activities. Community-oriented efforts have been directed toward particular targets, predominantly public or low-income housing projects. Overall, the objective has been to evolve a *balanced* program with equal emphasis on community or society-based problems on the one hand and personal or family-based problems on the other.

During the year and a half of reaching for—and partially incorporating—greater program diversity, new pressures and new choices have arisen for staff, administration, and board. Staff now want the board and administration to legitimize in a formal way the rapid and extensive changes that have already occurred in their practice. To do so requires fresh assessment of more or less traditional services in the light of expanding demands in the newer areas of community-oriented services, because major new money and resources are not available to ease the discomforts of having to make difficult choices.

I believe you would be interested in the exploration of more precise choices that the agency's supervisory group had to make and the rationale for these choices. Because these opinions have not yet been presented to the board, I cannot predict their fate. They do reflect a thoughtful senior staff effort to translate general mandates for diversity and innovation into the difficult process of decision-making that may be ahead for our organization and perhaps for others. The following summary from a report prepared by the seven-member supervisory group may be illustrative:

> Our shared view is that Family Service Association has tended to develop as a multifocus agency, attempting to provide coverage service in a number of areas embraced by a long-standing, open-door intake policy.
>
> There is a fallacy in suggesting that we can, in fact, provide a coverage service in any but a small number of areas, in the

light of the multiplicity of possible service roles suggested in the direction of service report. This view is reinforced practically by the day-to-day service demands that the district supervisors become aware of.

We view the agency as having stretched its limited resources into so many service areas that any *further* flexibility or innovative capability is severely limited. "Pseudo-coverage" may even mask the real extent of social need.

Have our attempts at "pseudo-coverage" padded the inadequacies of the *publicly* supported services which have legislative responsibility to provide total coverage in their respective service areas?

Our assumption is that the voluntary family agency should devote the largest part of its resources to exploring the ways in which it can effectively meet the *residue of need that lies clearly outside the responsibility of the network of public coverage services or public utilities.*

The agency should take an experimental approach to test and demonstrate helping methods and service delivery systems with manageable test populations.

The remainder of the agency's resources should be devoted to a much reduced core of coverage service which clearly rests on family service expertise and which serves to legitimize the agency's role in relation to various communities— the service community, the United Appeal community, and the community of the public at large.

We define "the most vulnerable groups" as middle- and lower-income groups and those groups for whom no service is available. While other definitions have been considered, we believe that these groups are the ones *most* in need of our services.

In considering future programs, we distinguish clearly between "hard core" and "adaptable" services. By "hard core" we mean those services which are ongoing; reflect our central expertise; and where we provide as much of the public service as is feasible in the absence of the public sector's effective implementation of comparable or better services. By "adaptable" we mean those programs which are experimental, time limited, aimed at solving or seeking answers in specific areas, or exploring different approaches to the issues encountered in the hard core areas. For example, in the social action area and in community problems which impinge on family life, adaptable services will be clearly time-limited programs related to specific problems based upon defining client groups or specific target areas. Such programs might or might not have a treatment purpose. The criterion, rather, would be the contribution to the solution of a particular problem, or the search for different approaches to problems. Being experimental, there would be more than usual emphasis on research design and evaluation of results. These programs would be derived most frequently from experience with families served in the hard core program and would aim to demonstrate different approaches where counseling would not alleviate problems.

I have summarized the supervisors' views in some detail because they illustrate clearly the tensions—and some of the agonizing choices—that face the voluntary family agency under expanding demands of *quality, volume,* and *diversity.* Moreover, such demands cannot adequately be met in the face of a rate growth in *financial* resources which has little relationship to the rising tide of greater and broader expectations.

Obviously, we are deep in the midst of a *process*—a process not unique to one agency or community, but nonetheless difficult in the search for relevance today as well as tomorrow. Of a number of options which may be open, the option of choice will be that which blends innovation with continuity, quality with diversity, risk with discipline born of tested and evaluated experience. Achievable? Perhaps not. But the very effort of trying to reconcile some of the seemingly irreconcilables—*there* is the stuff of which relevant goals and sound programs are made.

Note

1. For a detailed description of the program, see Lucile Cantoni, Family Life Education for Public School Teachers, *Social Casework,* 50:407–10 (July 1969).

SOCIAL ACTION TO INFLUENCE INSTITUTIONAL CHANGE

David R. Hunter

Miles and miles of turgid sentences have been written and spoken about "change," and it may not be possible to contribute any additional enlightening or energizing statements. The subject is so important, however, that although nothing new may be expressed here, reiteration, reinforcement, and reemphasis are valuable because the forces tending to impede progress are constant and strong. It is important, too, to keep in mind the spirit of optimism that underlies this conference. Although we are surrounded by uncertainty and gloom on the path toward a human society, the fact that we are here means that, in spite of all the overwhelming obstacles, we think we can do something about them. Therefore, it is not a waste of time to discuss the ways of doing something.

The subject of social action to influence institutional change is too big and too unknown to delineate unequivocally and systematically the goals to be sought and the best

Reprinted from *Social Casework*, April 1970.

means to seek them. One cannot be certain how thoroughly people comprehend ideas presented by a speaker. Questioned about what someone has said in his speech, listeners often find that one or two points remain clear, but the essence of the speaker's powerful and well-developed total argument escaped them completely.

I am, therefore, going to make a number of points that do not necessarily flow smoothly in a crescendo of logic to a flashing conclusion. They are points, however, that I think anyone contemplating social action to influence change must review at the outset or along the way.

Confrontation and disruption

Do we confront or persuade; do we disrupt or cajole? In discussing social action these days, it is necessary to begin with this question. In a society in which issues have become so stark, so polarized and in which many bright and energetic people are not going to sit still any longer, each organization has to think about its own most appropriate style. The organization must consider how its personality and character best equip it to seek desired results, and it must adopt the appropriate methods to attain these results. It must consider the dangers of backlash. Finally, it must appraise the true objective of a course of action and any unexpected course it may take once it is launched.

As a matter of general principle, there can be no doubt that there may be occasions in a society when tense and uncomfortable confrontation represents behavior of a high social and human order. Confrontation in this context means the act of saying to the representatives of authority, "Hold on, we are going to violate the written or unwritten rules of conduct to change your policies or to make a point, because it is important enough to warrant such disruption of the established order when the normal means of communication are not working."

When those who are planning a strategy of social action

consider disruptive confrontation as one possibility, it is to be hoped that they will give it careful thought. They must consider the issue of sufficient importance; they must remember that confrontation cannot be employed frequently. They must know that, although confrontation can push toward desirable goals, it can also subvert those very goals. It can polarize groups and lead to situations amounting to civil war. It can shake people up or threaten them sufficiently so that they do take overdue positive social action. At the same time, confrontation can alienate potential allies and stiffen resistance. It can oversimplify issues so that even if a specific battle is won, a larger war may be lost or lost sight of.

To ask human beings to weigh these factors in advance is asking a great deal; how much easier it is to do after the fact! These factors must be weighed, however, if the exercise is to be more than a venting of frustration, a dramatic adventure, or an arrogant and foolhardy escapade. Confrontation does not mean merely occupying a building, blocking an entrance, or interrupting a speaker. There is the confrontation of complacency with facts. Government and industry made some moves toward automobile safety when they were confronted with the facts. Officials in public housing and urban renewal began to change policies when they were confronted with facts about some deleterious effects of those programs. This kind of confrontation should be employed much more widely.

When power is misused, the wielders of that power should be confronted with the fact that their abuse is known and will not be tolerated. When an encrusted institutional system is operating to the detriment of the people it affects, the leaders of that system need to be confronted with this knowledge. We may avoid these kinds of confrontation because criticizing people of power and prestige may make us feel uncomfortable. Yet, there are still many emperors who must be told they are not wearing clothes.

Working both sides of the street

There is not any one best course of social action to accomplish desirable change. Activists who adopt different methods or different styles may seem to be incompatible with one another, but they are not necessarily so. For instance, those who say they are working within the system may often be serving the same ends as those working outside the system.

An organism changes both because of what happens inside it and because of what happens outside it, just as an apple changes when there is a worm in its inside or a frost on its outside. The same kind of change can occur in an institutional system. The Family Service Association of America changes when there is ferment within and pressure without.

It is not at all inconsistent for the same group or even the same person to work both ways. One day you may sign a petition to your congressman or even picket his office. The next day you may help him draft a bill. The leadership of an institutional system may often be willing to change if only they knew how. The professional person or the nonprofessional change agent or the broker of change has an important role to play both in sensing and capitalizing on a readiness to change and in helping to effect the change by offering practical suggestions of substance.

Having something to say

Perceptive and determined social change agents should be able to sense when an institution's leaders are ready for change and should be prepared with an effective program. In fact, the social activist who has some programmatic ideas to start with and describes them clearly is, by that very fact, likely to move the change process along. One cannot, however, always rely on this happening. Inspired changes in contrast to serendipitous ones—have certainly occurred as the result of the vague articulations of a charismatic leader or the energizing of a dynamic, if programless, organization. Because it is not possible always to have a charismatic leader on the spot, it is far better to be able to specify not only the needs for change, but also the changes needed. To be able to do that entails work, discipline, and imagination. It also requires the combination of theory and imaginative construction. For lack of these, many noble change efforts have come to naught.

At the same time, an activist should not be condemned for not having a precise program. Although it is better to have program and policy recommendations, change efforts even without them are legitimate and can be effective. Supercilious advice to youth to go away and keep quiet until they can tell us what they want, therefore, comes with ill grace and is usually merely a device to get rid of them.

Recognition of other changes

One of the effective ways in which changers weaken their efforts is by failing to notice the nature of other changes taking place all around them in the total system and to speculate rationally about their future outcomes. Recently Buckminster Fuller predicted the shipment by air of autonomous dwelling machines and universal credit card-managed retail service systems that will reinstall, maintain, and remove by air the dwelling machines from anywhere in the world within hours. Peter Drucker in *The Age of Discontinuity* says that development of ocean resources will have as profound an impact on us as had the plow. New materials are no longer substitutes for steel, glass, and other materials. It is now possible to make materials to suit specific purposes; man's new habitat, megalopolis, will result in new technologies and new major industries. These things are all going to have an impact on the things of immediate and professional interest.

A few years ago somebody *could* have speculated that technology, government policy, and the inherent pull of cities were going to be responsible for large numbers of poor people moving to urban areas, and it would be wise to prepare for them. Somebody *could* have speculated that people like automobiles, and therefore there would be many of them causing congestion on the roads and in human lungs. Somebody *could* have speculated that people have a need to identify pridefully with their own groups as well as with the larger society, and support could have been given earlier to black group identity and initiative. Phenomena of this kind affect and in part shape the problems and conditions to which change efforts are directed. It is just not possible to anticipate *everything* or to know about what is going on in all sectors of human organization, but a failure to be as aware as possible of these other currents and cascades may make individual efforts ineffectual, out of cycle, counterproductive or, worst of all, impertinent.

The closed-circle syndrome

In spite of the revolution in communications, there is still an inexorable tendency for people to talk to and act on their own peers. The communications revolution has so far been a revolution of communications technology, not technique, although it is possible that the youth and encounter subcultures may be in some new territory.

Communication alone is not going to make all the difference, but it is one of the things that has to take place. There are vested interests on the scene; there are real conflicts that are not going to be wished or talked away. There are also extensive marginal areas of common interest that are not recognized as such either because people in different groups are not talking to each other or because these areas are considered to be in conflict when in reality they may not be.

I have recently had the experience of meeting on one day with representatives of an organization of welfare clients and on the next day with a big-business group. The recommendations of both groups for recasting the welfare system were almost identical; yet the common image of these two groups, often shared by themselves, is that they are in immutable conflict.

How much systematic, continuing, face-to-face communication among different interest groups about critical community problems has there been recently? Do social workers talk with school administrators as a group? Do lower middle-class and working-class whites talk with blacks, again as identifiable groups with group interests? Does the bar association talk with radical youth? Finally, does the chamber of commerce talk with street corner youth who have entrepreneurial aspirations? This process of breaking out of the confining circles of those you already know, those who speak your language, those whose common background makes even a contentious situation comfortable is very important for social action. The parties involved will, at the very least, learn something about each other. If they are in contention they will know their enemy better. They might, however, be surprised and find some ground for common cause, and the infusion of new perspectives might even lead to social invention. It is not easy to move outside of one's own tribe. It has to be consciously adopted as a useful technique of social action and then followed systematically.

The coexistence of radicalism and reformism

The suggestion that corporate attorneys might exchange views with radical youth raises the whole question of whether or not radicalism and reformism can coexist in an open society. Does a radical have to despise reformers? Does a reformer have to spend as much time discrediting radicals as reforming society? An open society has room for both; in fact, it should welcome both. My reasons will satisfy dogmatists of neither stripe. It seems unlikely that— even with as many crises as it has—our society is in a revolutionary condition. The chances, therefore, are slim that a truly radical restructuring of our basic systems of business, property ownership, and government will take place. Will the radical settle only for a complete and basic recasting of the system and starting all over again on a different basis? I would hope not. Important and profound changes can be made in all these systems that will bring our society nearer to economic and social justice for all. I would think the radical might count his work well done if he helps to push the polity toward these changes. I think he does push when he articulates and insists on many of the objectives that radicals now have. Man's reach must exceed his grasp, and radicals help to extend that reach.

If this thesis is true, the reformer can view the radical as an ally. The reformer is not a radical because he thinks there may be a viper in the radical's Utopia, or because he thinks the radical may too frequently overlook the inseparability of means and ends, or too arrogantly skirt democratic process, or because he is simply afraid. The reformer, nevertheless, should recognize that the radical does two things of importance. First, by straining to pull society to the outer edges, the radical stretches the center (which the reformer also wants to do). Second, by calling for drastic change, the radical forces others to reexamine critically their own assumptions and goals—an urgent requirement for any thinking person in these times.

Reformers and radicals *do* have a need to talk to each other. Reformers should not let society destroy radicals, as it has a tendency to do. Radicals should not burst with frustration nor wither in cynicism if their goals are not fully realized.

The importance of energy in social action

The importance of ordinary energy in successful social action is often overlooked. It is all very well to plan and enunciate unimpeachable prescriptions for change, but placing them in a nicely plastic-covered presentation before the body politic is not likely to get them very far. Winners keep moving. They do not get tired and stop in midstream. If one way does not work, they try another. They set impossible deadlines for themselves. If it looks as though the ends of a particular social action might be achieved in a year, they say they will do it in six months. The forces of lethargy may be the biggest single obstacle to overcome.

Sometimes movement, activity, and energy may be even more important than clarity of objectives and strategy. Precision in the definition of goals and strategies in the social arena is extraordinarily difficult to achieve. At a given time, it may be as important to infuse with energy a general thrust toward a somewhat vague goal as it is to define the goal with precision. Greater precision and even dynamism may arise out of the movement.

Let us consider the question of income maintenance in this country now. There are many different ways to insure an adequate minimum income to all. Although we are on the way to establishing some national policy on this matter, we do not yet know what it will be. In the past few years, however, there has been a great deal of energy that in itself has fostered real progress toward defining just what the policy will be. We did not all sit back and wait for someone to fill in the details before pushing for the general policy.

Accountability in social action

Social activists need to step back every now and then and appraise their efforts. It is too easy to adopt a course of action that appears logical and promising only to find that for one reason or another it does not work, or that circumstances have changed so much that it is no longer relevant.

An example of the need for relevant action is the push toward metropolitan government. For a long time political scientists took for granted the fact that metropolitan government is a good thing, and if people were educated about it they would vote for it. In area after area it was voted down. Finally the political scientists reassessed the situation and recognized that the group interests involved would continue to produce negative votes. They have not given up the objective, however, and now they are approaching it in a more sophisticated manner through pressures and alliances, functional restructuring, and federal bribery. The activists realized that one approach was not working, and so they assessed the situation and adopted new techniques and strategies.

The field of social welfare has perhaps been as loose in this matter of accountability as any other field. There has been some movement toward greater accountability, but there is still a long way to go in assessing accomplishments and failures as a guide to policy and practice, in applying performance standards, in measuring results instead of appearances.

Single-purpose or multipurpose change?

Nobody loves a fanatic except the manager of a baseball team. Fanaticism in the social activist can easily frustrate his worthy purposes. By his intense, usually humorless, insistence that upon his issue depend all other issues, the fanatic turns off the people he is trying to turn on. He either frightens or bores them. In a world of complexity, interplay, and interdependence, his single-mindedness reveals a lack of sensitivity to the systemic kaleidoscope within which his own issue is played out.

Fanaticism in social action is error on two counts—substantive and tactical. First, it blinds the agent to the way in which the elements in any social system influence one another, and he is characterized perhaps as noble, dedicated, determined, and sincere, but naive. The man who once said, "Give me public housing and the slums will go" we know now was in grievous error. No more is decentralization of the schools or maximum feasible participation *the* solution. Those who stake everything on getting more professionally trained social workers tend to overlook the multiple utility of the paraprofessional. On the tactical front the single-purpose fanatic spends his time recruiting troops for his campaigns, hawking his nostrum, and scolding those who deviate from his method. He rarely joins the battles of others because he does not see them as sufficiently important to warrant digression from his own crusade. If he would occasionally join the campaigns of others, he might find more recruits for his own campaigns. He would also reduce his vulnerability to his opponents.

One way of eliminating an opponent is to pin a label on him and dismiss him. One might call Henry George a single-taxer and then snicker at him. One might call Carrie Chapman Catt a feminist and laugh at her. If the social activist works for more equitable taxation as well as for higher welfare grants, for opening up the suburbs to blacks as well as for gilding the ghetto, for lower tariffs as well as for lower caseloads, for minority business development as well as for family allowances, he is likely to find his credibility, his stature, and his effectiveness enhanced.

The brokerage role of the professional

Most of the people at this conference are professional people or semiprofessionals. They also represent a profession whose main concern is the human condition. The role of broker in social change is admirably suited to social workers. Few other groups have such natural opportunities to move around among different sectors of the community, to understand the views and requirements of different groups, to know what is going on here and what is going on there, and to assess individual and group capacities to accomplish specific goals.

For many social workers, therefore, the best role may be as broker rather than as leader or front-line trooper. The broker in social change may be required to push here or to prod there, to suggest a target or a strategy to a group in motion, to recognize potential allies and introduce them to each other, or to interpret the incomprehensible petitions of one group to another that must act on them or at least get out of the way.

This sort of action will not win medals or testimonial dinners, but the broker will be missed when he is gone. In today's environment of alienation, polarization, and gaps of one kind or another, it is the broker who may save us and keep us in fact moving forward.

Doctor, heal thyself

Nobody likes to be told how to straighten up and fly right, especially when the lecturer himself is not flying very well. Therefore, when agents of change are working to improve other organizational systems or to get others to do better, they will be well advised to examine the workings of their own institutional systems and, if necessary, straighten them out. With social workers this point does not require belaboring. The experience of recent years has been too painful. It was a rude shock for social workers to be told that perhaps their own rigidities, their blindness, and their vested interests were causing some of the trouble and that they should abandon their holier-than-thou posture.

We must keep in mind, however, that self-examination, self-criticism, and institutional analysis must be a continuing process if the agent of change is to have a solid platform and base of operation. Inviting other interest groups— clients, other professionals, lawmakers, youth—to help in such a process would prove that we practice what we preach.

Developing new perspectives

The problem of renewing our vision, of seeing things from new perspectives, of noticing new dimensions is a constant one. Most of us do not really worry about this problem very much or do anything about it; we plod along in the same old ruts and habits. We determine what something looks like, what we think about something at an early stage of our lives, and we tend to stick with it at all costs. That pattern is not good enough these days for anyone and certainly not good enough for the social activist.

To do something about a problem requires conscious will and the need to question regularly one's whole array of intellectual and perceptual equipment. It requires looking at things through the eyes of others, which in turn means getting out and meeting and talking seriously and deeply with others. It means asking outsiders to examine and criticize one's own system. It means pretending to start from scratch and building in fantasy a new structure or a new way to do something, unencumbered by what is already there. The fantasy might become a better reality.

These are some of the elements that will influence the kind of social action that may be undertaken and the outcome. There are many other questions that could be discussed. How can professionals and lower-class non-professionals work better together to accomplish common objectives? How can the law be used more effectively to bring about social change? How does one decide when to push, when to draw back, when to cajole, when to scream, when to seek allies, when to act alone? How does one avoid oversimplification in mobilizing widespread support? When does one set an idealistic, perhaps unrealizable, goal to inspire, and when does one become more pragmatic and incremental?

In conclusion, it may be helpful to shift from technique to substance. All the fancy techniques in the world do not make much difference if one is not working for something important. Our society is beset by very big problems, such as the war, the dehumanization of modern technological society, the inequitable distribution of wealth and power, the continuing exclusion of minority groups, the alienation of many intelligent and concerned youth, and the incapacities of present governmental structures. Let us hope that our social change energies will be directed to these basic problems and not wasted on peripheral niceties.

PLANNING FOR CHANGE
WITH NEW APPROACHES

Michael J. Kami

Before I present my ideas on planning for change, I would
like to discuss briefly the change in the environment, the
process of change as I see it. I am not a sociologist. I am
not a human behaviorist. I am not even an amateur psychiatrist. I am not any "ist" other than a pragmatic realist.
I am an ex-businessman turned fisherman and boat captain,
and I live in Florida. I can, therefore, only describe the change
as I see it, and I want to tell it without any institutional,
political, racial, or any other bias.

For years I have been fascinated by the physical change
that has been proliferating throughout this world. I have
watched the inventions, the discoveries in the fields of
physics, electronics, chemistry, medicine, computer technology, and the two-edged discoveries in the field of atomic
science. Bigger and bigger technological breakthroughs
occur in a shorter and shorter time interval. It took man

Reprinted and adapted from *Social Casework*, April 1970.

100,000 years to reach a speed of one hundred miles per hour. It took him one hundred years to reach 1,000 miles per hour and ten years to reach 25,000 miles per hour. The same accelerated speed of change we now encounter in the field of explosives, in the field of space, and in the field of computers.

Let us assume that there is an auditorium filled with about 800 people. If we create a game and consider that each of them represents one era or one lifetime in the history of humanity, we would have a span of approximately 50,000 years. This would be a very interesting assemblage of people, because 650 of this group would be cavemen or an earlier species of mammal. Only seventy would have any effective means of communication. Only six would ever have seen the printed word. Only four could tell time with any precision. Only one would have lived through every material progress and every invention that counts today. The next person to join that audience would see in half of his or her lifetime greater change and discovery than has been achieved in the whole history of 50,000 years of human civilization.

The knowledge explosion

One of the key reasons for this extraordinary increase in change is our knowledge explosion. If we measure the amount of knowledge man had 1,969 years ago at the birth of Christ and keep doubling that knowledge, the first doubling of knowledge was reached by the year 1750. The second doubling took only 150 years to the year 1900. The third doubling, which is eight times the amount of knowledge man had at the birth of Christ, took fifty years to the year 1950. The fourth doubling, which is sixteen times, took ten years to 1960. The fifth doubling, which is thirty-two times the amount of knowledge, took six years to 1966. By 1970, we have the sixty-fourth doubling of human knowledge, and it has occurred in four years' time.

No wonder life on this planet of ours gets very complicated, very complex, very incomprehensible, and very frustrating. Whereas technological change is revolutionary in nature, occurring in leaps and bounds, man's adaptation to this change is evolutionary because man thinks that way. Man's mind and emotions and living habits do not change at the pressing of an electronic or atomic button. We continue to have and to create gaps—gaps between technology and sociology, gaps between man, the machine, or man, the institution, and man, the human being. These gaps are many different kinds but they have one common element: They provide us with an increasing, not decreasing, number of problems with which we have to learn to cope.

Many growing gaps

We have a managerial gap and the managerial gap is growing. As business becomes increasingly complex, the ability to manage—to devise better systems of operations, control, and feedback—become more difficult because these systems are not keeping pace with the expansion of knowledge, products, and services that we are creating. Thus, business is experiencing great difficulty in training and creating new managers and better managers.

We have an institutional gap. Our institutions grow because the country grows—particularly governmental institutions become larger, more unwieldy, more bureaucratic, and more full of red tape. The delays in action, therefore, are increasing at a time when action should be accelerated.

We also have a talent gap. We need talented, innovative people in all fields to reverse the trend of the growing gaps. We have to reverse the trend of bureaucracy, inefficiency, and complacency. Large companies and institutions, however, find it more and more difficult to attract, hire, keep, and nurture talented people.

Then we have the standard of living gap. It is particularly apparent in the developing and underdeveloped countries. I should like to cite three examples of very complicated situations that are occurring throughout the world—situations that we are not really solving and that are going to cause many problems in the future.

I was recently in Japan, which has been enjoying an un-precedented boom in its economy and has thus become a major power. It has the world's third largest gross national product, which is increasing at the rate of 10 to 15 percent. Unless something happens to the economy in Japan, it is going to surpass the United States gross national product in about ten to fifteen years. The individual Japanese citizen, however, does not enjoy commensurate benefits because, although Japan is third in gross national product, the stan-dard of living—the per capita consumption—places Japan as twentieth in the list of nations. This fact means that the entire Japanese economy is geared for export and not for domestic absorption. An economic and social disaster may develop unless something really is moved around.

India, after forty years of progress and billions of dollars of aid, of investment, and of technological help, today has less food per capita than it had in the 1930s under British colonial rule. Here we have the problem of population explosion and the possibility of a major famine in Asia about the year 1972 or 1973 when probably 20 million people will die of starvation.

African nations and other severely underdeveloped coun-tries are in a seething turmoil because a shrinking world has created a wide network of communication that has per-mitted the underdeveloped countries of the world to see how the other half lives. At the same time, however, these nations have not enjoyed commensurate progress in their own standard of living, and they have little hope of achiev-ing the standards of the Western world.

Keeping up with change

In our own country we have many gaps with which we are all familiar. We have the racial gap, we have the generation gap, and the very dangerous pollution gap that may have a profound effect on future generations and on humanity's survival. The rate at which we pollute our atmosphere and our waters and absorb toxic chemicals from our soil and food is greater than the rate at which we are combating these dangers. The longer we wait, the bigger the gap and the bigger the problems we will have to solve.

The pollution of Lake Erie, the Hudson River, Chesapeake Bay, and the coastal areas and the smog over Los Angeles constitute a national disgrace. Large corporations, politicians, and private interests are disregarding existing laws and preventing the enactment and enforcement of new ones that may make a difference.

As social workers, you are actively engaged in alleviating human tragedies and human suffering and in helping many American families. You could easily add to my list other gaps of change that we have to bridge: the housing gap, the education gap, the medical services gap, the ghetto gap, the talk versus action gap, and the underprivileged children gap. What can we do about it all? How can we plan, program, and initiate meaningful action to start closing the gaps rather than just maintain the status quo?

Despite the fact that I have painted a gloomy but realistic picture, I am optimistic about the future. In fact, I am more optimistic today about society's ability to improve than I was several years ago. I believe that people are searching for true interests and true concerns and that there is real willingness to change things for the better. I think that people are finally beginning to try to reverse the trend of the growing gaps.

Each era in history, in recent history, has had its distinct characteristics. The 1930s during the Depression was the era of the politicians; the technology involved large mass construction. The 1940s was the age of the generals; the technology was the development of atomic power. The 1950s was the era of the businessman; the technology was the creation of large enterprises and the growth of the corporation. From the scientific point of view, it was the era of the discovery and the development of the computer.

The 1960s was the era and the age of the scientist; the technology was the conquest of space, the development of rocketry, and the walk on the moon.

What then will be the era of the 1970s? I believe—I hope realistically and not idealistically—that it will be the era of the human being. The key influence will be wielded by the educators, the social scientists, and the psychologists. The scientific endeavors of the 1970s will focus on human needs: education, help for the underprivileged, exploitation of the oceans for food and natural resources, and preservation of mankind through control and rehabilitation of polluted air and water.

It can be done, it must be done, but it will not be easy. Some 450 years ago Niccolo Machiavelli said, "There is nothing more difficult to take in hand, more perilous to conduct, or more uncertain in its success, than to take the lead in the introduction of a new order of things." We must introduce a new order of things. We must follow a system of planning for change that matches the rate of change.

Risk for the future

I would like to explain briefly a system that I think may make a difference in planning for change. I call it the *risk* concept of planning—R I S K. I have given this system the code name *RISK* because the element of risk is essential in any planning and endeavor. In any field, on any matter in today's world, we cannot have a program, we cannot plan for the future unless we accept a great element of risk.

A sure thing does not exist. A sure plan is a plan of yesterday that can as well be filed in a wastepaper basket. It is necessary, therefore, to stress the importance of taking a risk, of gambling, and of being prepared for failures.

The future is unpredictable and will become even more unpredictable as the number of variables grows in a shorter and shorter time period. Thus, the only thing about the future that we can be sure of is that it will not be the same as the present. It will not be a straight projection. It will not be a straight extrapolation from today's facts. It will be an unknown element and we shall have to take risks to prepare for it.

REVOLUTION
Many persons now expect an *evolution,* but they are going to get a *revolution.* R is the first letter in *revolution;* R is also the first letter in *RISK.* R also stands for *revolutionary* planning and not *evolutionary* planning for the future.

I used to have a trademark when I gave speeches at Arden House and addressed some of the people from FSAA. My trademark was a series of gears—a large gear, a smaller gear, and so on. I also had a series of wheels—from a large wheel to a small wheel. I used to say, "Gentlemen, this is my universal organization chart. The chairman of the board is the big wheel, the president is the smaller wheel, and the vice-president is an even smaller wheel. Then we have the regional manager, the district manager, and the branch manager; the senior salesman and the junior salesman." Finally the punchline was, "When I move the chairman of the board half a turn, the poor little fellow on the bottom revolves twenty-six times."

People laughed and salesmen roared and presidents rolled in the aisles. I no longer use that prop; I retired it on a shelf in my den along with a Stevenson button and a scientific treatise proving once and for all that the four-minute mile was beyond human endurance. Why did I retire it? Because I said that when the chairman of the board revolves, this poor fellow revolves twenty-six times, but if he tries to move, nothing happens. He will not move the chairman of the board. Today, however, the situation is different in a company, in an institution, in even a nonprofit organization. When the chairman tries to move, nothing revolves down below, but when the little guy moves a little, the chairman revolves twenty-six times.

This difference symbolizes the revolution. We used to manage people by the concept of *tomorrow*. We used to say, "You start working tomorrow and some day you will get better pay. In thirty-five years, you will get a gold watch and be able to retire in Maine, and we will give you a life insurance policy that is going to increase until it is so high that you cannot afford *not* to die working for us. You are going to get a bonus if you do a very good job, and we will give you stock options so that we catch you and you stay for years." The word is no longer *tomorrow;* the word—the key word—is *now.* Today people don't want tomorrow.

The young man wants his pay *now.* He does not really care about the large benefits from corporations because he is not going to stay with them for thirty-five years. He wants the bonus in advance. He wants to be able to say, "Trust me. Why should I trust you?" He is committed to the principle of *now.*

I do not consider myself a judge, nor am I saying what is wrong and what is right. I am trying to explain why there is a great deal of confusion about managing and understanding people on the part of stable, conservative, intelligent corporate officials, government officials, institutional officials, or any other officious officials.

We have a personnel revolution, and perhaps the boards of directors of many of the nonprofit organizations and the volunteers have to understand the R, the *revolutionary* concept of planning for the future rather than the *evolutionary* planning for the future.

There is also a moral revolution in the United States, and we have to understand it. Social workers probably understand it very well. A recent Harris poll, published in *Time* magazine, indicated that "immoral acts" committed by the establishment are viewed as much worse by far than the acts committed by the antiestablishment. This view is held by more and more people who stress the individuality and oppose the institution. A dramatic switch in public opinion happened in about a year's time. It was the switch from the hawks to the doves, the switch to the changing morality, the switch to being for the underdog rather than for the establishment.

INNOVATION

The second letter of *RISK* is I, and I stands for *innovation*. The ways, means, methods, procedures, thinking processes, or policies we have been using successfully up to now are obsolete, and they must be changed, improved, and transformed into innovations. If the rate of change increases and our way of operating does not match that rate of change, our way of operating becomes obsolete. I am not suggesting a change merely for the sake of change. I am suggesting a change for survival of the corporation, the organization, and the institution.

Innovation must become a way of life. Each of us must constantly ask himself, How can I do things not better, but twice as well or three times as well with the same resources? What can I change? How can I find a new way in every endeavor from the smallest task of getting mail faster in the office to the major efforts of establishing programs that are municipal, state, national, and international in nature?

There is more risk in not innovating than in innovating. Complacency that exists in institutions is very dangerous. Large corporations and the super-growth corporations know this well. They say that if they do not innovate, they will not grow; and if they do not grow, they will die. They must innovate because of their desire for growth and profits and because of the need to consider stockholder interests. The nonprofit organization has to adopt this same principle of innovation. It must prepare and present new products and new services in a different way and at a faster pace. Even if the products and services are adequate for *today,* the best thing would be to make them obsolete ourselves by introducing new methods for *tomorrow.*

Welfare counseling agencies should double their rate of introducing innovations; otherwise, they will not be serving their clients. I recommend innovation committees and innovation groups at all levels whose whole point of view and whose energies would be devoted to the question, How can we do the new things better according to the change around us? Above all, we must fight the bureaucracy, the red tape, and the delay, all of which are going to strangle us in the same way as they sometimes strangle the increasingly larger corporations and the increasingly larger institutions.

Alexis de Tocqueville wrote 134 years ago that "America is a land . . . in constant motion. . . . The idea of novelty is . . . indissolubly connected with the idea of amelioration. No natural boundary seems to be set to the efforts of man; and . . . what is not yet done is only what he has not yet attempted to do."

SYSTEM
The S in *RISK* stands for *system*. The system concept is now an accepted word in the terminology of the scientist, of the psychologist, of everybody. In order to be really meaningful, however, it also has to be simple. As life gets increasingly complicated, we must at least think in simple terms because simplicity in itself is complicated. What is a system? A human body is a system. All the organs are connected by the nervous system, a communication network controlled by the brain—the computer—and motivated by a goal, an ambition, a challenge. Each organ is dependent on another and cannot function independently. No single service, no single product, no single effort of an agency or a corporation is basically valid per se or alone.

People may forget what a system is. What good is it to build a bigger and bigger airplane, at the cost of billions of dollars, that in a few years will take hundreds of people across the Atlantic in two hours? This is not a system of transportation because what we want is not a bigger airplane. Let us suppose we want to go from a suburban home in the United States to a friend's home near London. What we care about then is a system of transportation. What good is it to be able to spend only two hours to cross the Atlantic when it takes an hour and a half to get to the airport, an hour to check in, an hour to wait for air traffiic control, two hours to circle on the other end, one hour to wait for the lost luggage, and two hours to fight the traffic into the city? We can cross the Atlantic in two hours, and we wait eight hours to do it. In other words, we have total travel time of ten hours which is more time than was required six years ago. We need to think always in terms of a system from the beginning to the end.

System planning for transportation must include roads, mass transit, ticket and luggage check-in, escalator and airport transportation, passenger and luggage loading and unloading. What is most important is to have a worldwide air traffic control to accommodate the giant airplanes safely, or we may very soon create the biggest air crash disaster in our history. Then probably we will wake up and we will produce a safe air traffic control system. Unfortunately, a traffic light is usually placed on a traffic intersection after a child has been killed but rarely before.

When someone mentions the word *housing,* I do not think of it as housing. I think of it as a system for living. Poor families may not need houses. They need a system for opportunity, such as vocational training, so that they qualify for jobs. Poor families need job opportunities to apply the skills they gain through vocational training. They need family counseling for their mental stability and happiness, and they need child guidance for their growing youngsters. They need day care centers to take care of the small children when both the man and wife work.

They need budget counseling to learn how to spend their money more intelligently. They need diet and medical counseling to keep healthy in order to be able to work. They need transportation to get to and from their jobs. They need good shopping facilities in the system for living so as not to be exploited by unscrupulous merchants. Of course, they need housing, but perhaps if all the parts in a true system for living were provided, they could afford and find living quarters for themselves. To think in relation to a system, every action, every program must be viewed in relation to the sum total of the parts.

KNOWLEDGE

The last letter of *RISK* planning, K, stands for *knowledge*. Since man's knowledge has doubled in the past four years, every one of us during these four years has become obsolete or at least obsolescent, unless we have doubled the amount of knowledge we have. Companies hire young people not because they have any prejudice against older people, but because they do not find in them the will power and perseverance to keep up with continued self-education that is essential in order to be a living part of society.

I believe very strongly in what John W. Gardner calls self-renewal. I call it periodic mental reincarnation, and I believe that every one of us in every field of endeavor must try to double his specialized knowledge and reincarnate his mental outlook or he will become useless to himself and to society. Thus K for knowledge in planning means homework, individual study of the latest techniques and discoveries in one's field of specialty.

It also means knowledge of the newest techniques that help in planning, including understanding of computers. Whether or not one likes these monsters, they are here to stay and they can be helpful. We must learn what computers can do for us and what they cannot do. We have to understand the compiling and exchange of statistical, demographical, socioeconomic data. Some of it will be available through computer memories or through communication networks. We must scan the environmental horizon for clues of change rather than facts. By the time we have all the facts, the environment has already changed, and then we are too late with our understanding. It is called paralysis through analysis.

Mistakes of the powerful

I would like to cite three examples of large, powerful, unique organizations that have missed the clues, the hints of change. The first one is General Motors. General Motors, under Alfred Sloan, with all the books written about its great organization and efficiency, has missed the boat because it misunderstood public opinion. Many years ago Charles E. Wilson, ex-president of General Motors, was the secretary of defense. He said, "What is good for General Motors is good for the United States." That remark evoked all kinds of jokes. Recently, however, General Motors has been shaken up by Ralph Nader, who exposed unsafe features of some General Motors automobiles. The power of public opinion was able to change an entire policy of development of that powerful corporation and to demonstrate that it cannot impose its will on the public.

American Telephone and Telegraph, one of the greatest and most efficient monopolies in the world, also missed the clues of change. Customers have been complaining about service, and, instead of responding with better service, telephone company representatives tell us about buying the Princess telephone that comes in seven delicious colors. The company projected the growth of telephone usage in various parts of the country as 10 to 15 percent when the actual growth was about 40 percent. The result has been a great decline in the efficiency of telephone service. In New York there are many delays and wrong connections. There may be a wait of seven to nine months for telephone installation by Southern Bell in Florida. It can take five days to get a repairman to come. The biggest federal investigation of American Telephone and Telegraph is about to be started. The mistake of AT&T was underestimating the rate of change.

The latest very interesting mistake is that of the highly organized Roman Catholic Church. It was efficient, it was worldwide, and it worked. Yet there was a miscalculation in not reading the signs of change, and the central top organization does not now get the same obedient reaction from all parish priests or from all parts of the world. There is a feedback and dialogue which did not exist in 1,969 years.

It is interesting that in matters of organization, of forecasting, and of public opinion, even large and powerful organizations can make mistakes by not feeling the wings of change. I am proud to be part of the corps of "effete snobs and intellectuals" who are not afraid of new ideas, new challenges, confrontations, and free speech.

Conclusion

The principle of RISK planning for change involves an awareness of *revolutionary* change, commitment to *innovation*, use of *systems*, and keeping abreast of new *knowledge*. We must set up *revolutionary* objectives that we really want—even if at first we do not see how we are going to get them—and compare them with the evolutionary changes that we would get normally. We need to create challenges in every department, in every work, in our personal lives, in agencies all over—create personal challenging gaps that we want to bridge.

Then we must try to fill the gaps with *innovative*, new, vibrant proposals—not just ideas but proposals. We need three times as many ideas as can be used because risk planning does not mean 100 percent success.

We must think in terms of a *system*—how do the parts of a plan interrelate? All parts must be considered—apparent, latent, organizational, community.

Knowledge of all new developments in a field and periodic mental reincarnation or renewal are essential to all planning if it is to be meaningful for the future.

RISK planning has worked in very large profit-making organizations. It has worked for thirteen corporations, which were the only ones of hundreds of thousands of corporations that have achieved sustained year-after-year supergrowth and superprofits. It should work for nonprofit organizations to achieve supergrowth and superservice for the betterment of mankind. Above all, we need to have a clear and determined philosophy. Reinhold Niebuhr stated it clearly, "O God, give us serenity to accept what cannot be changed, courage to change what should be changed, and wisdom to distinguish the one from the other."